What the Bible Says About Stewardship

YOU ARE IN CHARGE OF GOD'S GIFTS TO YOU

A. Q. Van Benschoten, Jr.

Judson Press ® Valley Forge

WHAT THE BIBLE SAYS ABOUT STEWARDSHIP

Copyright © 1983
Judson Press, Valley Forge 19482-0851

Illustrations with accompanying Scripture, texts and Scriptural quotations, unless otherwise indicated, are from the *Good News Bible: The Bible in Today's English Version* — Old Testament: Copyright © American Bible Society, 1976; New Testament: Copyright © American Bible Society 1966, 1971, 1976. Used by permission.

Other versions of the Bible quoted in this book are:

The Revised Standard Version of the Bible copyrighted 1946, 1952 © 1971, 1973 by the Division of Christian Education of the National Council of the Churches of Christ in the U.S.A., and used by permission.

The New English Bible, Copyright © The Delegates of the Oxford University Press and The Syndics of the Cambridge University Press 1961, 1970.

Library of Congress Cataloging in Publication Data
Van Benschoten, A. Q.
    What the Bible says about stewardship.
    Bibliography: p.
    1. Stewardship, Christian—Biblical teaching.
2. Nature—Religious aspects—Christianity—Biblical teaching. 3. Missions—Theory.
    I. Title.
BS680.S78V36   1983   248'.6   82-21373
ISBN 0-8170-0993-0

09 08 07 06 05
8

CONTENTS

You Are In Charge

Under the God of History[a]—Creator, Lord (Master, Owner), Redeemer

Prehistory Genesis 1:1	Ancestors Hebrews 1:1	Prophets Hebrews 1:1
Creation	2,000 B.C.　　900 B.C.	850 B.C.　　400 B.C.
Creation	Abraham[c]	Amos
Adam and Eve[b]	Jacob	Micah
Cain and Abel	Joseph	Hosea
Noah	Moses	Isaiah[d]
Tower of Babel	Joshua	Jeremiah
	David	Malachi[e]
	Solomon	

[a] "In the past God spoke to our ancestors many times and in many ways through the prophets, but in these last days he has spoken to us through his Son. He is the one through whom God created the universe, the one whom God has chosen to possess all things at the end" (Hebrews 1:1-2; also see Isaiah 41:4; 45:1a; 6,13a; Amos 9:7).

[b] As a steward, you are responsible to CARE FOR ALL CREATION. "I am putting you in charge . . ." (Genesis 1:28). "You appointed him [humans] ruler over everything you made; you placed him over all creation" (Psalm 8:6).

[c] As a steward, you are responsible for God's MISSION TO ALL PEOPLE. ". . . through you I will bless all nations" (Genesis 12:3b).

[d] ". . . I will also make you a light to the nations—so that all the world may be saved" (Isaiah 49:6b).

[e] "Bring the full amount of your tithes to the Temple . . ." (Malachi 3:10a).

Jesus Hebrews 1:1		Chosen to Proclaim 1 Peter 2:9	
A.D. Jesus[1]	30 A.D.	30 A.D. Philip Peter[9] Paul	Consummation

[1] "Go ... to all peoples everywhere. ... to the end of the age" (Matthew 28:19-20).

[9] "But you are the chosen race, the King's priests, the holy nation, God's own people, chosen to proclaim the wonderful acts of God" (1 Peter 2:9a).

Note: Each section of the above *time line* will be found in more detail at the beginning of each appropriate chapter.

INTRODUCTION

In recent years many people have experienced great uncertainty about there being any purpose for life in our time. This uncertainty appears to rise out of the turbulent worldwide political and economic situations which we have been experiencing. People often doubt whether there is to be a future. Is there really any hope? We know more about our whole world than ever before and have even ventured into space. We know that we can destroy the world by means of our latest scientific achievements. Of course, we can also improve the quality of life by our achievements.

Will humans destroy the world slowly through exploitation of its resources and pollution of the environment or quickly through war and nuclear weapons? Or will the world's time and life be extended and improved by planning for use of resources (stewardship) to sustain and improve life for everyone and by sharing God's Good News of redemption and reconciliation meant to bless all people? The issue has been posed in this form to give stewardship and missions their proper relational position. We are beginning to understand that stewardship means caring for all of creation. The present world condition—the growing numbers of people and the limitations of resources—challenges humans to deal with the stewardship of the whole earth as assigned by God at the time of the creation.

There is a tendency in the church to think of missions as its purpose for being. This emphasis came to the forefront with the modern missionary movement, which began in the late eighteenth century. The specific beginning of the modern missionary movement is usually cited as the year 1792, when William Carey of England went to India as a missionary. There was a great acceleration of mission activity following Carey's going to India. During the thirty years after 1792, many mission societies were organized in Europe and the United States, and missionaries were sent to many different countries. Also, Bible societies were organized to provide Bibles and Scripture portions so that new Christians could learn to read the Bible in their own languages.

Now it is time to place stewardship in its important overall position and not to think of it as just raising funds for the church. The stewardship movement has been a twentieth-century phenomenon which began with an emphasis upon giving money for the support of the church's local mission and its wider mission. The United Stewardship Council, the predecessor of the Commission on Stewardship of the National Council of the Churches of Christ in the U.S.A., began in 1920. Several Canadian communions participate in the Commission on Stewardship. The wider scope of stewardship responsibilities relating to the whole creation is being perceived and emphasized during the latter third of the twentieth century.

The Bible is the important book to which the churches look for guidance in life and mission. Christians especially look to the New Testament. While the commission given by Jesus of Nazareth to go to the whole world with the Good News is in the New Testament, the Old Testament also includes the expression of God's purpose for the mission of God's people. The matter of stewardship is found clearly in both Testaments. The first stewardship assignment to humans came at the time of creation (Genesis 1:26-29). The mission for God's people is closely related to God's covenants and promises and is related to God's concern for the whole world. It was first clearly stated in the covenant with Abraham (Genesis 12:1-3).

It is impossible to separate mission and stewardship completely. To discover the total scope and history of God's purpose and actions, we must look at the whole Bible. This book will help the reader to understand the biblical story of God's stewardship assignment to all people, the mission directive for God's people to go to all people, and the meaning of these for today's church. Both stewardship and mission will be seen in the relationships of God with the people, in God's action in history, and in a culminating purpose for history. Throughout history we will see God's concern for the whole creation.

The people of God do not always act in obedience and often fail in their understanding of God's purpose for them. Yet, the story is there in the Bible to help us understand and to encourage us to act as good stewards of resources and sharers of the faith. God's purposes are still valid, and God's presence provides our hope for a future. Though the Bible is complex, a unifying theme does run through it. The theme is one of redemption and salvation and revolves around the idea of a people of God who are called to live under God's rule and the related hope of the coming kingdom of God.[1]

Throughout the Old Testament there is a focus on God's consistent concern for all people. This was expressed through dealings with all people in Genesis 1–11. Following Genesis 11 the concern was expressed through a people chosen to be a blessing to all others. The Exdous event rescued these people from bondage in Egypt. The return from Babylon brought a few back to the city of Jerusalem. Then later God acted through Jesus Christ and the church, sending the church in mission to all people.[2]

The total stewardship required of human beings includes telling and sharing with all peoples the story of God the Creator, Owner (Lord), and Redeemer. These terms describe qualities that are observable in Jesus Christ and the Good News about Jesus of Nazareth. Though this study will take a look at many biblical texts about stewardship of resources and mission, it does not include an exhaustive list of texts. It is interesting to note that Psalm 24:1 is usually used by those discussing either stewardship or mission. To that extent it is a pivotal text for discussions about stewardship of resources and mission.

> The world and all that is in it belong to the Lord;
> the earth and all who live on it are his.
> —Psalm 24:1

Definitions of stewardship must include how humans live in the world and use its resources and must include the mission to the whole world. Following are four definitions:

> Christian stewardship is the dedication of all I am and have, under the control of God's Spirit in Christ, to the doing of his will, in recognition of his lordship, in gratitude for his love, in every area of my life, and in the service of his redemptive fellowship.[3]

> Christian stewardship is man's grateful and obedient response to God's redeeming love, and is expressed by using all resources that Christ's mission in the world may be fulfilled.[4]

> Christian stewardship is the working out of what it means to be the people of God in and for a world in rebellion against its Creator.[5]

Stewardship conceived in depth . . . is no less than
- the care and nurture of life
- the healing of one who fell amongst thieves
- the feeding of the hungry
- the freeing of the oppressed
- the befriending of the friendless
- the equitable distribution of earth's bounty
- the passion for justice and peace
- the dialogue with all who hunger and thirst for authenticity

Stewardship thus conceived is not a build-up of influence, power, property. It is not storing up possessions. It is not a head-count of converts. Stewardship is working for what God . . . seeks, in great humility, to being about: the peace, abundance, and glory of the creation. By God's grace we are empowered to serve. So stewardship is not an option. It is a total attitude. It centers the Christian upon the world God loves.[6]

The first definition uses the masculine pronoun in reference to God, and the second one uses *man* in the generic sense. Both usages are not acceptable in our time. But both definitions have historic and current value in understanding stewardship. The second definition is being replaced. The third and fourth definitions are helpful statements carefully worded.

The stewardship and mission of the church in this age must deal with ecology *(oikology)* and stewardship *(oikonomia).* The church is God's people, each one of whom is a steward *(oikonomos);* together we must fulfill God's plan (in other words, provide stewardship) for the whole universe. Though we tend to think of "the church" in general, it is helpful to relate these thoughts to the local churches, especially our own church.

Questions and Statements for Study and Reflection

1. Spend five minutes with each word, *stewardship* and *mission,* writing down every thought that comes to mind. After you have finished reading this book and have done the suggested study, either alone or in a class, do this exercise again. Compare your first thoughts with the later ones. What similarities and differences do you see? If you are in a group situation, you may wish to discuss the similarities and differences.

2. Spend five to ten minutes writing out your own personal statement

of life commitment. You may wish to do this again at the end of the reading and study and compare the two statements.

3. Following are four statements or affirmations on stewardship which have been revised to bring the language into acceptable form for today *(Studies in Stewardship* by the American Baptist Churches Division of World Mission Support, n.d.):

Stewardship Affirmation 1
   God is the Creator and Owner. God is Giver, Redeemer, and Sustainer of all.
   Genesis 1:1–2:4a; 12:1-3; Psalm 24; Colossians 1:15-23; Hebrews 1:1-3.

Stewardship Affirmation 2
   Each person is a steward; all he or she possesses is a trust from the Creator.
   1 Chronicles 29:1-18 (especially vv. 14 and 16); 2 Corinthians 8:1-9; 1 Corinthians 4:1-5; 1 Peter 4:10-11; Isaiah 42:5-7; 49:6; Luke 2:28-34a.

Stewardship Affirmation 3
   Each person must acknowledge his or her stewardship before God in this life.
   1 Corinthians 4:2; 6:19-20; Luke 12:48; 24:45-49; Acts 1:6-11.

Stewardship Affirmation 4
   Each person must ultimately give an account to God of his or her stewardship.
   Genesis 3:9,11; Isaiah 45:23–46:5; Luke 16:1-13; Romans 14:10-12.

Try writing one or more affirmations on the *mission* of the church. The preceding affirmations on stewardship provide a model. These affirmations on stewardship and those that you write on mission can be used again and again by the church in worship and commitment services.

4. As you read the *Daily Bible Readings* listed at the beginning of each chapter, make notes of themes that you find there. Also, watch for the repetition of themes.

1

IN THE BEGINNING GOD

Daily Bible Readings

1. Before the World Was Created, the Word
    John 1:1-5; Colossians 1:15-20
2. The Story of Creation and the Consummation in the New
    Heaven and the New Earth
    Genesis 1:1–2:4*a;* Revelation 21:1-7
3. The Garden of Eden and the New Jerusalem
    Genesis 2:4*b*–3:24; Revelation 21:9–22:5
4. God the Creator Is to Be Praised
    Psalms 8; 104; Hebrews 2:5-9
5. The Earth and All of Creation Is the Lord's
    Psalm 24; Colossians 1:15-23
6. Humans Created to Be Like and Resemble God
    Genesis 1:26-27; 2:7-8, 18, 21-23
7. Humans Put in Charge of the Creation
    Genesis 1:26, 28*b;* Psalm 8:6-8; Luke 12:41-48;
    16:1-9; Mark 13:34-36

IN THE BEGINNING GOD
Genesis 1:1

Prehistory

Creation: Genesis 1:1–2:4*a*

Adam and Eve: Genesis 1:26-31; 2:4*b*–3:24

The Stewardship Commission for All People: Genesis 1:26-28
    "I am putting you in charge . . ." (Genesis 1:28).
    "You appointed him ruler over everything you made;
    you placed him over all creation" (Psalm 8:6).
    The theme of this stewardship commission can be
    worded as follows: CARE FOR ALL CREATION.

Cain and Abel: Genesis 4:1-26
    ". . . placed under a curse . . ." (Genesis 4:11*a*).
    ". . . went away from the LORD'S presence and
    lived . . . east of Eden" (Genesis 4:16).

Noah and the Flood: Genesis 6:1-9ff.
    "But the LORD was pleased with Noah" (Genesis 6:8).
    God's covenant with Noah: "never again will a flood destroy
    the earth" (Genesis 9).

Tower of Babel (Babylon): Genesis 11:1-9
    ". . . build a city . . . make a name for
    ourselves . . ." (Genesis 11:4).
    "The LORD scattered them . . ." (Genesis 11:8).

IN THE BEGINNING GOD

Genesis 1:1

The opening words of the Bible, "In the beginning, when God created the universe . . ." indicate clearly that God was perceived by the Hebrews as the God and Creator of all that is in heaven and earth. This universality of God's relationship to all creation can be understood as the basis for believing that God has a concern and purpose for all peoples, for all creation.

At the very beginning of the Christian's book of faith, the Bible, are two stories of creation (Genesis 1:1–2:4a and Genesis 2:4b–3:21). In Genesis 1:26-28 God is described as having said, ". . . we will make human beings; they will be like us and resemble us. They will have power over the fish, the birds, and all animals, domestic and wild, large and small" (1:26). Then after the male and female were created, God blessed them and said to them, "Have many children, so that your descendants will live all over the earth and bring it under their control. I am putting you in charge of the fish, the birds, and all the wild animals" (1:28). The words "I am putting you in charge . . ." are exceedingly important. These words express the fact that God showed concern for creation by placing human beings in charge of that creation. They are to take care of it. To be in charge is something like being the foreman on a ranch. The foreman does not own the ranch. He or she is in charge of the operation and is responsible to the ranch owner. The foreman is a steward. In biblical times a steward was a person put in charge of someone else's property. One Canadian church body has said, ". . . Stewards (or the Board of Managers) supervise the temporal affairs of the pastoral charge."

In the second creation story a "Garden of Eden" is developed as a part of the whole universe made by God (Genesis 2:4b,8-14). "Then the LORD God placed the man in the Garden of Eden to cultivate it and guard it" (Genesis 2:15).

A similar expression of the Hebrew understanding of God, the creation of humans, and the human position of responsibility in the world under God is found in Psalm 8. The psalm begins (and ends) with the words:

> O LORD, our LORD,
>   your greatness is seen in all the world!

The psalm continues:

> What is man, that you think of him;
>   mere man, that you care for him?
> Yet you made him inferior only to yourself;
>   you crowned him with glory and honor.
> You appointed him ruler over everything you made;
>   You placed him over all creation:
> sheep and cattle, and the wild animals too;
>   the birds and the fish and the creatures
>   in the seas.

The psalmist understood well the human being's place in God's economy—stewardship.

"You are all one in union with Jesus Christ" (Galatians 3:28).
". . . I am putting you in charge . . ." (Genesis 1:28b).
". . . chosen to proclaim the wonderful acts of God . . ." (1 Peter 2:9).

The wonder and awe of the creation is not made much of in the

Western world. This may be true because of the awe the Western world holds for what humans have discovered through science. In some cases there is a disbelief in a creation by God. In the Christian's religious experience the emphasis has been so much on the great revelation and redemptive act of God in Jesus of Nazareth, the Christ, that the previous history of God's acts among people is not given much attention. Fred Denbeaux, who wrote about creation in *A Handbook of Christian Theology,* attributes the lack of concern and interest in creation during the Reformation in the sixteenth century to an emphasis upon Jesus the Christ. He wrote:

> The historical task of the Reformation was to direct attention not to the creation but to the Creator, not to the order of the world but to the faithfulness of Him who had redeemed it.
> A high price was paid for this victory. Although new vigor was given to the doctrine of redemption, the idea of creation was all but lost.[1]

From boyhood days I have wondered about the church's lack of emphasis upon the Old Testament. The emphasis seemed to be largely upon the New Testament. Several years ago while visiting with a hospital chaplain in a Christian hospital in Thailand, I became aware of the excitement felt in the Christian community about the creation stories found in the Old Testament. The non-Christians there held that the world had always existed, and they had no concept for God. That Thai Christians felt great excitement about God and creation added impetus to my own interest in the Old Testament. Reviewing God's action in the Old Testament, God's concern for all people, and God's covenanting with a people to share that word of concern with all other people has helped to complete and make even more significant God's action as recorded in the New Testament—the Good News about Jesus Christ's redeeming new creation of persons, the coming new age (the beginning of which is now), and the new heaven and the new earth in the future.

To be reminded of the creation story is to rediscover the nature of human beings, their likeness to God, and their immediate responsibility to God, the Creator, for the world. Humans have responsibility for the whole creation. God is Lord over humans. God gave this stewardship assignment. The fact that this was the first assignment made would appear to point up its importance.

Being in charge of the whole world is the subject of a 1971 Commission on Stewardship tract:

man: you're in charge

"Man!"
God called out to Adam,
"have dominion over this world I created.
Be fruitful and multiply!
Explore it
Dig in it
Fly over it
Enjoy it
and remember
I give you authority over it and
responsibility for it.
In short, Man,
you're in charge!"

"All of it?"
asked Adam incredulously.

"All of it!"
replied God firmly.

"The fish in the sea?
the fowl in the air?
the beasts in the field?
and the land and the water?
and the land under the water?
and . . ."

"All of it!"

"Wow! Lord!"

Down the ribbon of Time
Adam and all his begotten kin
have taken turns
accepting authority and responsibility;
some men have
harnessed the fire
conceived the wheel
developed engines
designed wings
while others have
drilled for oil
dug for coal
refined for tools
probed for light
searched for health.

Some who've assumed dominion have

held authority preciously,
provided responsibility responsibly;
some
grabbed authority
but fumbled responsibility.
Some became authority
and ignored responsibility.
Some listened to God
while others turned deaf ears to Him.

Today
God still calls out:
"Man! Have dominion over this world I created!
Explore it
Probe it
Fly over it
Conquer it
Subdue it
Enjoy it
I give you, Man,
authority and responsibility for it.
In short, Man,
you're in charge!"

"Over all of it?"
we ask incredulously.

"All of it!"
is the resounding answer.

"The fish dying in the sea?
birds fluttering in the air?
beasts moaning in the fields?
and the raped land?
the stagnant air?
the fouled water?
and . . . ?"

"All of it!"

"Forgive us, Lord!" [2]

Following the creation events in the early chapters of Genesis, we have the stories of Cain and Abel (with the older brother killing the younger), Noah and the Flood (with the "rainbow promise" by God at the end), and the Tower of Babel, or Babylon (with the scattering of people all over the earth, speaking in different languages and making communication difficult). Anger led to murder; wickedness and continual evil thoughts led to the destruction of the earth, which was escaped only by

Noah and his family; and the arrogance of reaching to the sky to make a name for themselves led to the separation and alienation of the people. These events all led to the beginning of God's redeeming action of covenanting with one people to tell God's Good News for *all* people.

God's covenant with Abraham is taken up in chapter 12 of Genesis. This second assignment by God to a "chosen" people was preceded by the first assignment to all people to be in charge of all creation. Dr. Douglas Hall of McGill University, in lectures to the ecumenical Commission on Stewardship of the National Council of Christian Churches in the U.S.A. in December, 1979, stated that stewardship is primary and that Christian mission flows from stewardship.[3]

Questions and Statements for Study and Reflection

1. Think through the meaning of "being in charge" *(Good News Bible)* or "having dominion" (King James Version) over God's creation.

2. In our day what does having charge of the universe mean in relation to mineral resources, use of water and land, disposal of wastes, use of the oceans and seas, care of the forests, use of interplanetary space, etc.? These issues should be thought of in the context of the relationships and rights of peoples in our own time and also the relationship of the peoples of our time to future generations.

3. What perception and understanding do you have of God as the owner of the universe and its resources? What does this perception say to you about your relationships to the things of this universe?

4. In each of the four stories of Genesis 1-11, find the acts of humans that are thought of theologically as being sinful. List them. What was God's action or attitude in relation to the acts of humans?

5. In the Noah story consider the significance of the concepts of disobedience, obedience, salvation, covenant.

6. Read the following editorial and consider the questions at the end of it.

The Ways of the Tree
Reflections on Psalm 145:15-16
By A. David Stewart

There once was a tree whose beauty and splendor were a joy for all to see. It was known far and wide and there seemed to be no other tree quite like it in the whole world.

The tree was ever-changing from its glistening freshness in the morning sun to its soothing sway in the breeze at day's end. Likewise, the beauty of the tree remained through the changing seasons, from the new life of spring . . . to the full bloom of summer . . . to the glorious color of fall. In winter's rest the tree stood stately and serene. It was simply a magnificent tree.

Not only was the tree beautiful and magnificent. It was also a very generous tree. It was so generous, in fact, that it became home for many, many different kinds of creatures. Its strong branches offered perches from which the birds could sing their songs to the highest heaven. There were crevices in the tree which made for cozy nesting. The leaves from last year's harvest made the ground rich and fertile.

Each summer and fall the tree would open its storehouse and bring forth all manner of good things to the creatures around it. There was rich soil for worms . . . and worms a-plenty for robins . . . There were fat flies for the frogs . . . and scrumptious nuts for squirrels.

The tree was very happy about the creatures who made their homes around it and the community the creatures formed together. There was no greater joy and fulfillment for the tree than to care for every creature, each in a special way. The ways of the tree were very compatible to the creatures, and they lived together in happiness and harmony.

*   *   *

One day some of the creatures in the community began to ponder the ways of the tree. It was not long before they decided to make some changes which they thought would improve conditions in their community. Conditions were not all that bad; it was just that these creatures thought they could do some things to make life better. It is a natural thing for creatures to do, I suppose.

So, the creatures made their changes. Summer and fall were made so the tree's storehouse could stay open more days every year. Nets were spread under the branches to catch the falling leaves. These creatures felt leaves were only a nuisance and very, very messy as they lay on the ground, especially when the rains fell upon them. Some of the branches were tied together to allow these creatures to get to other parts of the tree more rapidly.

The experiment seemed to be working. In many ways the world of the tree had become neater and more luxurious. And the changes were so gradual that many creatures hardly noticed any change at all. But to others the changes were very obvious. The tree, still tall and stately, showed signs of fatigue. Its leaves hung limp. Its branches began to droop. The tree swayed much more in the evening breeze. Now that the leaves were caught by nets, the tree no longer got the nourishment it needed. The shortened winter rest made the tree very tired.

Neither did all the members of the tree's community [fare] so well under the new arrangement. The worms became smaller . . . which meant the robins became weaker, and their songs that cheered the morning grew faint. Other creatures became disoriented and confused. Flies were attacking frogs . . . the squirrels went nuts searching for good nuts! There was all manner of tension and conflict among the creatures who used to live together in harmony and happiness.

Those creatures who had made the changes were not [faring] so well either. Once vigorous, hearty and alert, they had eaten more, because the tree's storehouse was staying open longer each year. And they exercised less . . . and their minds had become dull. They no longer stopped and visited with other creatures on their long walks about the tree. Their short cuts had ended all of that.

Some of the experimenters began to ponder the ways of the tree. They were aware that all was not well in their community. Maybe their changes had not made life better after all. The tree had spent many, many years refining and perfecting its ways. Maybe the most magnificent and wonderful thing of all was the wisdom of the tree to give just enough to its creatures to keep them strong and happy and yet not too much so as to cause the creatures to have indigestion and all sorts of irritable disorders.

So branches were unbound . . . and nets came down . . . and leaves floated playfully to the ground once more. The tree is resting once again . . . the experimenters are exercising and finding long lost friends as they walk through the old neighborhood once more.

The ways of the tree are not only splendid and magnificent . . . beautiful and loving . . . The ways of the tree are wise and well.

Consider these questions:

a) What is the difference between natural change in nature and the changes caused by the decison of the birds?

b) Is there really happiness and harmony in the relationship of the birds and the tree (humans and the creation)?

c) Is it always possible to reverse the change made by the birds (humans)? If so, how?

GOD SPOKE TO OUR ANCESTORS

Daily Bible Readings

1. Life Is Sacred; Cain and Abel
   Genesis 4:1-16; Hebrews 11:4; 1 John 3:12

2. Disobedience, Obedience, Rainbow Promise
   (Covenant with the World)
   Genesis 6:5-21; 9:8-17

3. Arrogance Scatters the People Across the Earth
   Genesis 11:1-9

4. God's Call and Covenant with Abram (Later, Abraham)
   Genesis 12:1-9; 15:1-21; 17:1-8; Galatians 3:6-29

5. Moses Chosen by God
   Exodus 6:2-8; 19:4-6; Deuteronomy 7:7-10;
   1 Peter 2:9; Revelation 5:9-10; Hebrews 11:24-28

6. God Chose a People to Serve as Priests to the Whole Earth
   Exodus 19:4-6; 1 Peter 2:9; Revelation 5:9-10

7. Prayers for the Nations
   Psalms 67; 86:6-12; Revelation 15:2-5

GOD SPOKE TO OUR ANCESTORS
Hebrews 1:1

2000 B.C. **900 B.C.**

Abram (Abraham): ". . . through you I will bless all nations" (Genesis 12:1-3).
Another task in stewardship for God's people is to be in MISSION TO ALL PEOPLE.
"And Abram gave Melchizedek a tenth of all the loot he had recovered" (Genesis 14:20b).

Jacob: "They will be as numerous as the specks of dust on the earth. . . . through you and your descendants I will bless all the nations" (Genesis 28:14).
". . . and I will give you a tenth of everything you give me" (Genesis 28:20-22).

Joseph: Genesis 41:39-40

Moses: The Exodus Event—Exodus 6:2-8; 19:4-6
"The whole earth is mine , but you will be my chosen people, a people dedicated to me alone, and you will serve me as priests" (Exodus 19:5b-6).
"So now I bring the LORD the first part of the harvest that he has given me" (Deuteronomy 26:10).

Joshua: Settlement in the Promised Land—Joshua 24

David: 1 Chronicles 16:1-36; 29:1-19
"Everything in heaven and earth is yours. . . . all riches and wealth come from you . . ." (1 Chronicles 29:11b-12a).

27

"Yet my people and I cannot really give you anything, because everything is a gift from you, and we have only given back what is yours already" (1 Chronicles 29:14).

Solomon: 1 Kings 8:41-43

". . . so that all the peoples of the world may know you . . ." (1 Kings 8:43*b*).

GOD SPOKE TO OUR ANCESTORS

Hebrews 1:1

There were numerous covenants made by God with Abraham, Moses, and David in the Old Testament and with the people through Jesus of Nazareth in the New Testament. We have named the two sections of the Bible, the Old Testament and the New Testament (covenants). There is a tendency when thinking of the Old Covenant to think first and foremost of the Mosaic Covenant made at Sinai. This may be because it is related to the Exodus deliverance, which is mentioned again and again as the mighty redeeming act of God and also as the symbol of God's promise of deliverance through the Messiah, Jesus of Nazareth. The Mosaic Covenant and the Davidic Covenant both speak of God's dealing with the people as the messengers for God to the nations of the earth. In future reading, watch for any ideas or declarations which seem to point to the convenant with Abraham as being the more significant—grace of God, faith of humans, blessing for all nations.

The covenants are made by God, who is recognized as sovereign, and often speak of blessings or curses based on obedience or disobedience. Scholars have read many treaties of the Old Testament period in which the winning rulers formally stated their relationships with the conquered rulers and people. In these ancient treaties we find one or more of the following elements: (1) preamble, (2) historical prologue, (3) stipulations laid on the conquered, (4) provision for a public reading of the treaty and a place to put it for safekeeping, (5) a list of divine witnesses to the treaty, and (6) blessings and curses for keeping or breaking the treaty.[1] Look carefully at the covenants mentioned in these pages for any of these six elements that were found in the suzerainty treaties of the Old Testament historical period.

The call of Abraham and the covenant promise to Abraham, with the implied responsibility of Abraham and his descendants, signal God's provision for the possible restoration of all living beings to a right relationship with God. This call is the beginning point for the Hebrew people's understanding of themselves as a chosen people, chosen for the purpose of being a blessing to *all* people and a witness that God has not abandoned *any* people. Abraham lived before the time of the giving of the Law; so this relationship of Abraham and God was understood to be by the grace of God and is recognized to be so in the rest of the biblical story. The covenant included a command to go, the promise of another land, the promise of many descendants, and the promise that through Abraham and his descendants there was to be a blessing for all the nations of the earth.

> The LORD said to Abram, "Leave your native land, your relatives, and your father's home, and go to a country that I am going to show you. I will give you many descendants, and they will become a great nation. I will bless you and make your name famous, so that you will be a blessing.
> I will bless those who bless you,
> But I will curse those who curse you.
> And through you I will bless all the nations."
> —Genesis 12:1-3
(See also Galatians 3:8, 16, 19 and Romans 4:13.)

This covenant with Abraham was affirmed later by the promise of a son and again by the promise of land (Genesis 15). Still later an affirmation was given in the sign of the covenant—the promise that the covenant would be everlasting (Genesis 17). God declared again in Genesis 18:17-19 that Abraham would have many descendants and that they would be a blessing to all nations. In part, God said, "I have chosen him in order that he may command his sons and descendants to obey me and to do what is right and just. If they do, I will do everything for him that I have promised." In the hour that Abraham was ready to offer his son to God, God repeated his promise (Genesis 22:15-18).

In the midst of this period of the original covenant, affirmation of the covenant, and additions to the covenant, Abraham pursued four kings in an effort to rescue his nephew Lot. He returned with Lot and all of the recovered stolen goods. He was met by Melchizedek, king of Salem and a priest of the Most High God, who praised God for the victory of Abraham. In the midst of this time of praise, Abraham ". . . gave Melchizedek a tenth of all the loot . . ." (Genesis 14:20). This is the first biblical record of a tenth (tithe) being given. It surely was already a common thing to do. Abraham did it quite naturally, and he probably did it in recognition of the fact of Melchizedek's priesthood and in honor of the Most High God, who Melchizedek said ". . . made heaven and earth . . ." (Genesis 14:19).

All through the Old Testament there is a tension between the human tendency to exclusivism and God's universalism. The Hebrews tended to withdraw from all others and to think of their position as a special one in God's sight. God always indicated that his interest was in all peoples. God's purpose was for the Hebrews to be a blessing to all the world, and take God's message of love and salvation to all peoples.[2]

Joseph, a great grandson of Abraham, had an experience in Egypt which has great importance in illustrating the story of God's redeeming action. The description of Joseph's appointment by the king (Pharaoh) to handle the administrative matters relating to seven years of plenty and seven years of famine exemplifies clearly the relationship of God and humans in the stewardship appointment found in Genesis 1:26-29.

> The king said to Joseph, "God has shown you all this, so it is obvious that you have greater wisdom and insight than anyone else. I will put you in charge of my country. . . . Your authority will be second only to mine" (Genesis 41:39-40).

When people from all over the world came to Egypt to buy grain (Genesis 41:57), Joseph's brothers also came to buy grain. Joseph's interpretation of God's hand in history helped to remove the tension felt by the older brothers and thus established Jacob's descendants in the history of the concept of "redemption" (Genesis 45:4-8). Joseph's stewardship assignment from the king, as it was carried out fully, led to a reunion of the whole family of Jacob and the reconciliation of Joseph with his older brothers.

Stewardship assignments can be narrow and specific or quite broad. The wine steward was the person who told the king about Joseph, the Hebrew slave who could interpret dreams. Although Joseph was originally summoned by Pharaoh to interpret dreams, he was given the assignment to care for the country's grain supply for a fourteen-year period. God assigned human beings to care for all of creation forever. The process of stewardship calls for the steward to be responsible for an assigned task and also to be responsible to the one who made the assignment.

Several centuries later Joseph's stewardship action eventually led to the Exodus event. (See God's promise to Jacob in Genesis 46:1-4.)

Probably the mighty act of God that was most significant to the Hebrew mind was God's delivery of the Hebrews from slavery in Egypt.

When God called Moses to lead Israel out of Egypt, God did so with a reminder of the covenant with Abraham (Exodus 6:2-8). The Exodus event, referred to many times in the Old Testament and in the New Testament, was a landmark event and remains a symbol for many seeking liberation from a variety of oppressive situations in the twentieth century. A high moment during the Israelites' wandering in the wilderness was the Mount Sinai experience. Usually the Ten Commandments (Words) are thought of in connection with Mount Sinai. But in addition to giving the Ten Words, God also made a statement connecting the covenant with the deliverance from Egypt; the people were expected to be obedient and to be priests to the world. Serving as priests in the world would mean representing the peoples of the earth before God and declaring God's greatness to all people of the world. God, the owner of the whole earth, said,

> You saw what I, the LORD, did to the Egyptians and how I carried you as an eagle carries her young on her wings, and brought you here to me. Now, if you will obey me and keep my covenant, you will be my own people. The whole earth is mine, but you will be my chosen people, a people dedicated to me alone, and you will serve me as priests (Exodus 19:4-6; see also 1 Peter 2:9 and Revelation 5:9-10).

Israel could accept or reject the covenant. To accept the covenant brought responsibility and blessing. To reject the covenant brought a destroyed relationship, a curse. By the time of the writing of the book of Exodus, the Hebrew people were at least aware of God's intent that, as a chosen people, they had a mission in and to the world. The choice or election of one people was not a rejection of the world by God but a declaration of God's interest in all the peoples of the earth.

Near the end of his life Moses spoke at length to the people. He reminded them that the promise to Abraham and the deliverance from Egypt along with the Sinai Covenant were a part of their history. the deliverance was a means of being able to keep the promise to Abraham (Deuteronomy 7:7-11). Instructions were given for the day when the people would settle in the land and would want a king like other nations around them. The king would be chosen by God and would be one of their own people. The king would need a copy of the law to read and live by in order to remember that he was no better than anyone else (Deuteronomy 17:14-20). God was to be recognized as the supreme ruler even though the people had a king.

The recognition of God as the ruler and owner of creation is stated clearly in Leviticus when the year of Jubilee is described as the year in which all land was to go back to the original owner or family.

> Your land must not be sold on a permanent basis, because you do not own it; it belongs to God, and you are like foreigners who are allowed to make use of it (Leviticus 25:23).

People in fact possessed the right only to use the land and not to own the land. In another historical story the same point about God's ownership is pictured well when King Ahab of Israel recognized that even as king he did not have the right to take Naboth's vineyard by force. His queen, Jezebel, daughter of the king of Tyre and Sidon, had an entirely different understanding about the rights of a king, and she arranged to have Naboth killed so that the vineyard could be taken by Ahab (1 Kings 21).

In the ceremony of the annual harvest, Moses instituted a special harvest offering and called for a recitation in the central place of worship that would regularly remind the people of their deliverance from Egypt and their being led to the Promised Land (Deuteronomy 26:5-10). A further word in Deuteronomy 26:16-19 states God's recognition of the Israelites as a chosen people and God's call for obedience, which would bring praise and honor to God's name. There is no reference here to foreigners other than those who were present, celebrating with them. The presence of foreigners would surely have reminded the Israelites of God's purpose for them to be a chosen people, chosen to be priests and a blessing to the nations of the world.

Along with the mandate to offer the firstfruits of the harvest to commemorate the deliverance from Egypt, there was an admonition to give a tenth of the crop each third year to provide adequate food for the Levites, the foreigners, the orphans, and the widows. In this way God's goodness would be celebrated, and God's ownership of all things recognized. These offerings would provide for the house of God and feed the poor, who were so important in God's sight. Therein is found a part of what stewardship is about.

While the people were getting settled in Canaan, the Promised Land, Joshua, Moses's successor called all of the Hebrew tribes together to recite the story of God's promise to Abraham and to tell how God had delivered them from Egypt and brought them into the Promised Land.

Joshua then called for a promise from the people to serve God faithfully—a sort of covenant renewal service (Joshua 24). The covenant was written down and kept in the sanctuary at Shechem.

The period of time between the invasion of Canaan and the establishment of the monarchy was one of warfare aimed at conquering the

"When I defeat them, the Egyptians will know
that I am the Lord" (Exodus 14:18).

land, followed by a time for settling into the land. Fighting did not allow much time for attention to the Israelites' responsibility of being priests to the nations, some of which they were fighting. But the repeated paradigm of obedience, rebellion, punishment, and salvation reminded the people that God was still present and that survival, in fact, depended on their loyalty to God. Obedience was a required part of the covenant relationship of the people of God.

The story of Ruth is set in this time of the Judges even though it was probably written much later. The story demonstrates in a striking way that a foreigner who was faithful to the God of Israel would be blessed just as an obedient Israelite would be blessed. Ruth was one of those who benefited from the gleaning laws that God had given to help the poor have enough food. Ruth's husband-to-be was practicing his stewardship when he had his workers leave the corners and edges of the fields for the poor to harvest.

In the period of the establishment of the monarchy, the prophet Nathan told King David of God's promise that his dynasty would last forever (2 Samuel 7:1-17; Psalm 89:3-4, 28-36; and 2 Chronicles 6:16-17).

When David brought the Covenant Box (the Ark of the Covenant) into Jerusalem, the Levites led the worship service in front of it and sang a song of praise which included a proclamation to the nations of God's greatness. The song also contained a call for the people never to forget God's covenant with Abraham, which was made to last forever. Worship in the tent, and later in the temple, was to be a reminder of God's great covenant with Abraham and God's concern for the nations of the earth. God expressed a purpose for the people of God in the covenant with Abraham. The covenant with David was a promise of how God's concern for the nations would be fulfilled in David's line, in Jesus of Nazareth, the Son of God. Also in the same text is a reminder of God's covenant with Jacob promising him the land of Canaan as his possession forever (1 Chronicles 16:1-36).

At the time David designated his son Solomon to be his successor, he told the people that Solomon was to build the temple to God, which was to be a more tremendous job than building a palace. David described how thoroughly he had prepared materials for the temple and how much he was giving of his own personal property. Then he made an appeal: "Now who else is willing to give a generous offering to the LORD?"

Clan heads, tribal officials, army officers, and royal property admin-
istrators volunteered to give. The people gave. They were happy at the
size of the offering, and David was extremely happy as well (1 Chronicles 29:1-9). Out of that happiness David expressed an understanding
about God, power, and wealth:

> You are great and powerful, glorious, splendid, and majestic. Everything
> in heaven and earth is yours, and you are king, supreme ruler over all. All
> riches and wealth come from you; you rule everything by your strength
> and power; and you are able to make anyone great and strong. Now, our
> God, we give you thanks, and we praise your glorious name (1 Chronicles
> 29:11-13).

Such an understanding is the basis for the stewardship of human beings
before their God.

David, in what are reported as his last words, expressed his understanding of the promise of the continuation of his dynasty, sealed in an
eternal covenant (2 Samuel 23:1-5; Psalm 89). "The dominant idea in
Judah, from David's time on, was that God had promised the land to
Abraham by covenant and in a parallel way had promised dominion to
the line of David." [3]

Many of the psalms were written in the time of David and of Solomon.
(Others were written later.) More than a hundred and fifty references
to the nations of the world are to be found in the Psalms. These poems
and hymns, which were for use in private and public worship, were a
constant reminder that God is the God of the nations, that God created
them and expected worship from them. Two selections represent this
emphasis found in the Psalms.

> God, be merciful to us and bless us;
>   look on us with kindness,
> so that the whole world may know your will;
>   so that all nations may know your salvation.
>   —Psalm 67:1-2

> All the nations that you have created
>   will come and bow down to you;
>   they will praise your greatness.
>   —Psalm 86:9

Solomon at the dedication of the temple revealed his belief that God
would hear foreigners and that the Hebrews were to be the means for
peoples of the earth to recognize and know God. This implies that God

is the God of all the world. In his prayer Solomon said:

> When a foreigner who lives in a distant land hears of your fame and of the great things you have done for your people and comes to worship you and to pray at this Temple, listen to his people. In heaven where you live, hear him and do what he asks you to do, so that all the peoples of the world may know you and obey you, as your people Israel do. Then they will know that this Temple I have built is the place where you are to be worshiped (1 Kings 8:41-43).

It is implied in these psalms and in Solomon's prayer that the travels of the people of God would take the reputation of God to the nations of the earth and that people in those nations would pray to God and would come to Jerusalem to worship.

It is made very clear through the ancestors Abraham, Moses, and David that God is above all powers, is ruler of the earth, and intends the nations of the earth to be blessed through Abraham and his descendants. The world's resources are to be used to praise God and to care for those having needs.

Questions and Statements for Study and Reflection

1. What is your understanding of the significance of God's covenant with Abraham—for then and for now?

2. How is the Exodus event important to the Hebrew people, and how is it important to Christians in our time?

3. What is your perception of God as being active in history? How is that important to us in our time?

4. Make notes on how the elements of what God says to the Chosen People are similar to the elements of the suzerainty treaties. How does this information instruct our understanding of what God is saying to us now?

5. In a Bible dictionary find the description of the functions of a priest. Relate those functions to the mission of the Christian.

6. What new insights have you had concerning the fact that God is the creator and owner of all that is?

7. Does Abraham's giving of the tithe (10 percent) to Melchizedek

offer any guidance in stewardship functioning? What does it say to you?

8. How does the following sentence relate to God's commands about care of the poor and others in need? ''The needs of the poor take precedent over the wants of the affluent.''

9. As a stewardship mission/evangelistic responsibility and opportunity, what does it mean to *be a blessing to all people*? Consider this in relation to Genesis 12:1-3 and the phrase *mission to all people* used several times in this book as the second major stewardship responsibility, the first one being *care for all creation*.

3

GOD SPOKE THROUGH THE PROPHETS

Daily Bible Readings

1. God in the Midst of History
   Amos 9:5-8; Isaiah 41:4-5*a*
2. Justice and Righteousness Expected
   Amos 5:8-27; Isaiah 58:3-10
3. God Warns and Is Ready to Forgive
   Jonah 4; Matthew 6:12
4. Israel to Be a Light to the Nations
   Isaiah 42:5-7; 49:6; Luke 2:28-33
5. Servant and Suffering Servant
   Isaiah 42:1-4; 44:21-22; 53; Luke 9:21-27
6. A New Covenant
   Jeremiah 31:31-37; Luke 22:17-20;
   1 Corinthians 11:23-25
7. The Time of the End
   Daniel 12:1-4; Revelation 1:3-8

GOD SPOKE THROUGH THE PROPHETS
Hebrews 1:1

850 B.C.   **400 B.C.**

Amos: "The Lord says, 'People of Israel, I think as much of the people of Sudan as I do of you. I brought the Philistines from Crete and the Syrians from Kir, just as I brought you from Egypt'" (Amos 9:7).

Micah: "Many nations will come streaming to it. . . . Let us go up the hill of the LORD . . ." (Micah 4:1c-2).

Hosea: "What I want from you is plain and clear: I want your constant love, not your animal sacrifices" (Hosea 6:5b).

Isaiah: ". . . justice to every nation. . . . lasting justice to all. . . . God created the heavens. . . . I, the LORD, have called you and given you power to see that justice is done on earth" (Isaiah 42:1-6).

". . . not only will you restore to greatness the people of Israel who have survived, but I will also make you a light to the nations—so that all the world may be saved" (Isaiah 49:6).

". . . My Temple will be called a house of prayer for the people of all nations" (Isaiah 56:6-8).

Jeremiah: "The Lord said to me, 'I chose you . . . selected you to be a prophet to the nations'" (Jeremiah 1:4-8).

"I will make a new covenant with the people of Israel and with the people of Judah. . . . I will put my law within them and write it on their hearts . . ." (Jeremiah 31:31-37).

Malachi: "Bring the full amount of your tithes to the Temple, so that there will be plenty of food there. Put me to the test and you will see that I will open the windows of heaven and pour out on you in abundance all kinds of good things" (Malachi 3:8-10).

GOD SPOKE THROUGH THE PROPHETS

Hebrews 1:1

The selection or election by God of one people as the people of God was not a rejection of the other nations of the world. It was God's method for communicating to the world God's message of love and concern for all people and God's desire that people be in a right relationship with God. The prophets of the eighth, seventh, and sixth centuries B.C. spoke of God's covenant relationship with the Chosen People, who were chosen to be in this covenant relationship as declarers of God's concern for the nations. The prophets also told of God's sure punishment of the covenant people for being disobedient and rebellious. God expected obedience from the covenant people, the people of God. The fact that obedience to the covenant was more important than sacrifices is illustrated in a statement by Delbert R. Hillers concerning Hosea 6:6:

> . . . Hosea: "I desire loyalty, not sacrifice, and knowledge of God more than burnt-offerings" (Hosea 6:6). In others words, even the most lavish sacrificial ritual cannot replace fidelity to the covenant and its Lord, so the people cannot point to their observance of cultic forms as a substitute for obedience. . . . Finally, in Hosea's summary, they are to "walk" humbly with God.[1]

When one remembers the significance of the Exodus event to the Hebrew people as revealed through the many references to it in the biblical text—how it is the symbol for their deliverance, their political and economic liberation, and their salvation—God's message to the Hebrews through the eighth-century prophet Amos is startling. The Chosen People were being told that God was in the midst of the migrations of other peoples, too!

> The LORD says, "People of Israel, I think as much of the people of Sudan as I do of you. I brought the Philistines from Crete and the Syrians from Kir, just as I brought you from Egypt" (Amos 9:7).

The Hebrew people could not be complacent in their role as the "chosen" ones. God criticized them for their crookedness, greed, and self-seeking of personal comfort above the welfare of other human beings. God spoke of Israel's desire for the Day of the Lord and said there would be no hope in it for them because of their disobedience.

> One of the most creative moments in man's spiritual pilgrimage was when the great prophets of Israel became aware that God was uncontrollable precisely because he was really in control. The Hebrew people had settled themselves comfortably with the illusion that, because they were a chosen people it was up to God to look after his choice. . . . Hear the final shattering of all complacency—'Did I not bring Israel up from Egypt, the Philistines from [Caphtor], the Arameans from Kir?' [Amos 9:7, RSV].[2]

Micah was a contemporary of Amos. He also spoke of God's judgment on Israel and Judah, and he offered hope for a ruler who would come out of the small town of Bethlehem Ephrathah and who would rule his people well. The people would live in peace because peoples from all over the earth would acknowledge his greatness (Micah 5:2-5*a*). Micah also saw the peoples of the earth coming to Jerusalem to visit the temple of Israel's God.

> In days to come
> the mountain where the Temple stands
>   will be the highest one of all,
>   towering above all the hills.
> Many nations will come streaming to it,
>   and their people will say,
> "Let us go up the hill of the LORD,
>   to the Temple of Israel's God.
> For he will teach us what he wants us to do;
>   we will walk in the paths he has chosen.
> For the LORD's teaching comes from Jerusalem;
>   from Zion he speaks to his people."
>   —Micah 4:1-2

The words from Amos and Micah are a reminder that other nations have a place in God's plan. The prophecies were a preparation for the future New Testament emphasis on sending witnesses to all nations.

Another eighth-century prophet was Jonah. The Book of Jonah is an outright plea from God for mission to another nation, a nation that was a real enemy of the Hebrew nation. It was a daring act for a writer to make this plea from God to the Hebrews, who were so filled with nationalistic and religious exclusiveness. Jonah was calling his nation to remember that their God was the Creator of all that exists and was the absolute sovereign over the creation; therefore, God had a concern for all peoples. It was a call for the Hebrews to be a source of blessing to all nations as the covenant with Abraham said they would be. The Hebrew feeling toward another nation is expressed in the words of God in Jonah 1:1-2 and Jonah's brief message to Nineveh in Jonah 3:4c.

> One day the LORD spoke to Jonah son of Amittai. He said, "Go to Nineveh, that great city, and speak out against it; I am aware of how wicked the people are" (Jonah 1:1-2).

> Jonah started through the city, and after walking a whole day, he proclaimed, "In forty days Nineveh will be destroyed!" (Jonah 3:4).

The words of the response of the king of Nineveh in his proclamation to the city probably indicate that Jonah said much more than the few words recorded in the Book of Jonah (Jonah 3:6-9).

The attitude of the exclusive position the Hebrews felt they had and an understanding of God's universal concern for all people were both expressed in the words and actions of the man Jonah. First, Jonah revealed the attitude of exclusiveness held by the Hebrews by his reluctance to preach repentance in Nineveh:

> Jonah, however, set out in the opposite direction in order to get away from the LORD. . . . Jonah went on to tell them that he was running away from the LORD.

> The sailors were terrified, and said to him, "That was an awful thing to do!" The storm was getting worse all the time, so the sailors asked him, "What should we do to you to stop the storm?"

> Jonah answered, "Throw me into the sea, and it will calm down. I know it is my fault that you are caught in this violent storm" (Jonah 1:3a, 10-12).

> Jonah was very unhappy about this and became angry . . . . "Now then, LORD, let me die. I am better off dead than alive" (Jonah 4:1-3).

Second, Jonah had an understanding that God was concerned about other nations and their relationship to God. Jonah understood this, even though he had difficulty relating that understanding to his own life, just as Peter did centuries later (see Acts 10:34-36 and Galatians 2:11-14). Jonah said, "I am a Hebrew. . . . I worship the LORD, the God of heaven, who made land and sea" (Jonah 1:9).

> So he prayed, "LORD, didn't I say before I left home that this is just what you would do? That is why I did my best to run away to Spain! I knew that you are a loving and merciful God, always patient, always kind, and always ready to change your mind and not punish" (Jonah 4:2).

The message that the story of Jonah reveals clearly is that Israel should cease trying to run away from her destiny and should assume her covenant responsibility of proclaiming God to the nations.

Isaiah was another prophet of the eighth century, the century in which the Northern Kingdom, Israel, was overpowered and most of the people carried into captivity. In the first thirty-nine chapters Isaiah speaks of the rebelliousness of God's people and how they would be punished. There was also hope in his message, expressed in the sign of Immanuel (Isaiah 7:10-14) and in this promise: "The day is coming when the new king from the royal line of David will be a symbol to the nations. They will gather in his royal city and give him honor" (Isaiah 11:10). Although the emphasis is upon a Davidic king and Jerusalem as the center for worship, the Hebrews would perceive themselves as a people with a word for the nations, the story of the mighty acts of God.

The second part of Isaiah (chapters 40 to 66), which may have been written in the sixth century by another author, and the Book of Jonah, which hearkens back to God's originally revealed intentions, provide a glimpse of a future emphasis on God's concern for all people. Johannes Blauw has written:

> If *every* declaration of universalism in the Old Testament is called "missionary," then Isaiah 40–55 and the book of Jonah are indisputably the high points of the Old Testament from the missionary point of view. But, if the word "missionary" is confined to the idea of being sent out to the nations with the message of salvation, then these two portions of Scripture become almost the only passages in support of an idea of mission.[3]

Isaiah 40–66 has much to say about social justice for all people as the concern and task of God's people. They are to be a servant people, though sometimes the servant theme is illustrated by the description of an individual. Justice is seen as a loving concern for the well-being of people. The servant people were to bring justice to every nation. Surely that is mission. An understanding of justice for others grows out of one's recognition of God as the Creator and Owner of all things and the recognition of all persons as God's creatures. Isaiah 42:1-4 speaks of the servant people bringing justice to every nation. (See also Isaiah 44:21-22 and 52:13–53:12.) Isaiah 42:5-7 states that the Creator who has made all things has given to the servant people the power to see that justice is done on the earth; through the servant people God will make a covenant with all nations and bring light to all nations. (Also see Isaiah 49:1, 5-6.)

Though Isaiah 56:1-8 speaks of the Temple in Jerusalem, it is a statement on social justice and the individual's responsibility for practicing it. The foreigners who give allegiance to God are included in the family of God, which finds joy in the house of prayer. "My Temple will be called a house of prayer for the people of all nations" (56:7*b*). Isaiah's word from the Lord, relating to social justice and not unrelated to salvation, is very clear in 58:6-12, where he tells what religious fasting is, and in 61:1-2, the text quoted by Jesus at the beginning of his ministry. Jesus obviously meant this text to set the tone for his ministry of freeing people and saving them. To gain additional understanding of what needs correction in human relationships, the Scripture between these last two Isaiah texts should be read. The message is clear. Action is the message. The life-style is the message. Proclamation verbalizes the message.

In this latter portion of Isaiah God promises return of the people from the exile. One can say accurately that the return from exile in Babylon is another "Exodus" event. This mighty act of God is also another salvation experience for God's people, even if only a remnant of them are involved. In chapter 45 God declares that the world will know that God is the Lord when they see God working through Cyrus to return a people to Jerusalem. It is God who sets things right for the people.

> The LORD has chosen Cyrus to be king.
>
> "I do this so that everyone
>   from one end of the world to the other
>   may know that I am LORD
>   and that there is no other god."
>
> "I myself have stirred Cyrus to action
>   to fulfill my purpose and put things right."
>   —Isaiah 45:1*a*,6,13*a*

This Lord of history is in all history from the beginning to the end, from the creation to the consummation (see Isaiah 41:4).

In the latter part of the seventh century B.C. and the early part of the sixth century, just as Judah was falling, the prophet Jeremiah predicted that Judah would fall because of the evil ways of the people. But God promised that a remnant of the people would come back to Jerusalem. This was to be a captivity followed by a new exodus, another great act of God. Jeremiah affirmed that God was still present in the world and that Israel would be preserved as a nation forever under a new covenant, presumably to carry out God's purpose (Jeremiah 31:31-37). In Jeremiah 11:6-8 Judah is reminded of the covenant relationship and the fact that the people have not kept the covenant. Jeremiah's call was not just to Judah but to all the nations. The nature of God's word to Judah ensured that other nations would hear. Jeremiah wrote:

> The Lord said to me, "I chose you before I gave you life, and before you were born I selected you to be a prophet to the nations."
> I answered, "Sovereign LORD, I don't know how to speak; I am too young."
> But the Lord said to me, "Do not say that you are too young, but go to the people I send you to, and tell them everything I command you to say. Do not be afraid of them, for I will be with you to protect you. I, the LORD, have spoken!" (Jeremiah 1:4-8).

God's commission to Jeremiah told him where to go and what to say, and then it reassured him that he could expect God's presence with him. Note the similarity of the statement to the Great Commission given by Jesus in Matthew 28:19-20.

The prophet Daniel wrote in the apocalyptic style during time of stress that is thought to have been in the Babylonian exile period. Daniel witnessed for God as he served the foreign government. One can conjecture that the capitivity, with its scattering of the people, was a way for God to provide a witness to the nations. Daniel's vision in the eighth chapter speaks of the end times. This theme is picked up in the New Testament. The twelfth chapter tells of God's book of names—of those who will enjoy eternal life and of those who will suffer eternal disgrace. God promised Daniel that he would rise to receive his reward at the end of time. This, too, is a message more like the New Testament than the Old Testament. The old theme of doing what is right appears in a commendation of those who have taught others what is right. These teachers shine like a light.

> The wise leaders will shine with all the brightness of the sky. And those who have taught many people to do what is right will shine like stars forever (Daniel 12:3).

Compare this with Philippians 2:15*b* and also see Isaiah 49:6; 42:6; and Acts 13:44-48; 26:23.

Though the commission to go to the nations with the message of salvation may not have been spoken specifically in the Old Testament except Isaiah 40–45 and Jonah, there is much emphasis upon the people of God in covenant relationship with God as the means of blessing the nations. This was first declared in God's covenant with Abraham. Solomon's prayer clearly recognized God as one who hears all people. Micah spoke of all nations coming to God. Jonah understood God to be a forgiving God who related to all people, even Israel's great enemy, Babylon. Isaiah thought of the Hebrews as being the light to the Gentiles—proclaiming the good news and living a life-style of assuring justice for others and freeing the oppressed. Proclamation and presence together are the message. But the Hebrew people, to a very large degree, thought of God as the God of the Hebrews and considered Jerusalem, especially the Temple, as the focal point of their religious worship. The nations-will-come-to-Jerusalem syndrome afflicted the Hebrews seriously. After the prophets were no longer around to voice God's concern for all people, "Israel . . . signally failed to realize the generosity of God's purpose and the nature of its own vocation . . ." [4] Jesus, however, renewed the message of the prophets concerning God's universal concern for all people.

"Many of the exiles left the province of Babylon and returned to Jerusalem and Judah, each to his own hometown" (Ezra 2:1).

By the time of Jesus Herod had built a temple that was much larger than earlier temples and had an outer court. This outer court could be frequented by Gentiles and was sometimes known as the "Court of the Gentiles." This court was a fresh recognition of an old truth: Gentiles also have a place in God's presence and plans.

In the Old Testament the giving and sacrifice that were part of worship provided the maintenance of the place of worship and the support of the priests. The center of worship was the Temple in Jerusalem, and to it the peoples of the nations could come to worship and bring their offerings. There was scarcely any "sending out" in the missionary sense. A leading Old Testament text on the tithe and on support for the temple is found in Malachi 3:10, the often used "storehouse" tithe verse. It came in response to the question, "How are we robbing thee?" (3:8, RSV). There was a promise for the people who did bring the tithes and offerings. But even the promised benefits were to lead to a recognition by other nations of God's blessing on Israel. Good stewardship was to lead to a fulfillment of the mission God had given to Israel.

Some scholars writing on the biblical theology of mission speak of the Old Testament as *centripetal,* drawing the nations in toward God in Jerusalem. In the New Testament, mission is described by the same writers as being *centrifugal,* going out from Jerusalem to the nations.

Questions and Statements for Study and Reflection

1. What stands out as the prophets' message for Israel?

2. List the prophetic concepts or messages that seem to relate to the covenant with Abraham more than to the covenant with Moses.

3. List prophetic understandings of God's truth which *implicitly* and *explicitly* point to a mission for God's people in the world. Make two lists.

4. In what ways do you understand God as having a concern for all people? Is God also a forgiving God?

5. In what ways do you see the very presence of a person of God as a salvation message in contrast to the verbalization of that message?

6. In what ways can one speak of social concerns as having a relationship to salvation?

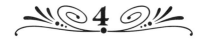

GOD SPOKE THROUGH HIS SON

Daily Bible Readings

1. The Lost Sheep of the House of Israel
   Matthew 10:5-15; 15:21-28
2. The Kingdom of God
   Luke 17:20-21; 20:9-18
3. The Great Commission—to the End of the Age
   Matthew 28:16-20; Revelation 22:6-17
4. The Commission—to the Whole Human Race
   Mark 16:14-18
5. Beginning in Jerusalem—Take the Message to All Nations and to
   the Ends of the Earth
   Luke 24:45-49; Acts 1:6-11
6. So Send I You
   John 20:21-23
7. I Pray for Those Who Believe Because of Their Message
   John 17:1-26

GOD SPOKE THROUGH HIS SON
Hebrews 1:1-2

Jesus: Gospels and Early Acts

"Go . . . to all peoples everywhere . . . to the end of the age" (Matthew 28:18-20).

"Go throughout the whole world and preach the gospel to all mankind . . ." (Mark 16:15-16).

". . . and in his name the message about repentance and the forgiveness of sins must be preached to all nations . . ." (Luke 24:45-49).

"Peace be with you. As the Father sent me, so I send you . . ." (John 20:21-23).

". . . witnesses for me . . . and to the ends of the earth" (Acts 1:8).

". . . in order that the world may know . . ." (John 17:20-23).

Jesus: God's People to Be One/with a Purpose

"How terrible for you, teachers of the Law and Pharisees! You hypocrites! You give to God one tenth even of the seasoning herbs, such as mint, dill, and cumin, but you neglect to obey the really important teachings of the Law, such as justice and mercy and honesty. These you should practice without neglecting the others" (Matthew 23:23).

". . . remembering the words that the Lord Jesus himself said,

'There is more happiness in giving than in receiving'" (Acts 20:35).

"Do not be afraid, little flock, for your Father is pleased to give you the Kingdom. Sell all your belongings and give the money to the poor. Provide for yourselves purses that don't wear out, and save your riches in heaven, where they will never decrease, because no thief can get to them, and no moth can destroy them. For your heart will always be where your riches are" (Luke 12:32-34).

"This is my body" (Mark 14:22).

GOD SPOKE THROUGH HIS SON

Hebrews 1:1-2

A lthough the first three Gospels and Acts were written later than most of Paul's letters, and the Gospel of John even later, we will look first in this chapter at the Gospels and the opening words of Acts.

Jesus was concerned first with the people of Israel when he sent out the twelve disciples to preach and to heal (Matthew 10:5-15). The disciples' support was to come from the people to whom they went. They were to tell the people, "The Kingdom of heaven is near!" This was the Good News; the new age proclaimed by the prophets had arrived.

In his ministry Jesus related to non-Jews as well as to the people of Israel. Luke reports the story Jesus told of the good Samaritan, which teaches that even the shunned Samaritans were people of worth (Luke 10:30-37). Jesus himself talked to the Samaritan woman of the village of Sychar. The story of the prodigal son has meaning for everyone— Jew and Gentile. Jesus commended the Roman centurion for his faith. The parable of the wicked tenants (Luke 20:9-18) implies that the kingdom is also for others than the tenants who destroy and kill. Jesus said that his house, the Temple, was a house of prayer for all nations. His story on the final judgment in Matthew 25:31-40 teaches of a final day when history will be consummated and the people of all nations will be gathered before the judge. The division of the nations will not be made on the basis of Jew and Gentile but on how one treats the hungry, the thirsty, the stranger, the sick, the unclothed, and the prisoner.

A large portion of each Gospel is about the final days leading up to Jesus' death, burial, and resurrection. During the last week, the Lord's Supper (Communion, Eucharist) was instituted in the upper room. In each recording of this event (Matthew 26:26-29; Mark 14:22-25; Luke 22:15-20 and 1 Corinthians 11:23-25) Jesus declares that the cup is God's new covenant, sealed with his blood. The cup and the loaf symbolize God's redeeming act through Jesus Christ and stress the covenant relationship with God. This redeeming act of the death of Jesus is one of the mighty acts of God that is to be proclaimed. It is the culminating and supreme act of redemption. In some ways this is a third Exodus as people are saved from their sins. This Exodus is different in that it focuses, not on Jerusalem, but on the whole world. It is a salvation from what could have been a Jerusalem captivity.

All the Gospels culminate in the pronouncement of the resurrection of Jesus and the call to mission emerging from it. Each of the commissioning statements of Jesus occurs after the resurrection.

> The resurrection, as the crowning of Christ's work, is *the* first and great presupposition and condition for the proclamation of the gospel among the nations. The second is the gift of the Holy Spirit. . . .[1]

Each commission is for the disciples to go to the whole world (Matthew 28:18-20; Mark 16:15-16; Luke 24:45-49; John 20:21-23; and Acts 1:8). In Acts 1:8 Jesus indicates that the people must wait in Jerusalem for empowerment. The bearing of witness is to begin there and move out to the whole world.

> "But when the Holy Spirit comes upon you, you will be filled with power, and you will be witnesses for me in Jerusalem, in all of Judea and Samaria, and to the ends of the earth" (Acts 1:8).

These words are a response to the question "Lord, will you at this time give the kingdom back to Israel?" Jesus' response in the commission is a clear indication that Israel and Jerusalem are no longer to be the focus of God's attention and the center of religion. Jesus is now the focal point. The direction of mission is away from Jerusalem to the nations of the world. The sovereignty rests with Jesus. "I have been given all authority in heaven and on earth" (Matthew 28:18). The imperative is to "make disciples" for Jesus. The process of mission is going out to the world, making disciples, baptizing them, and teaching them. To be involved in God's mission is to be involved in the whole mission, not just one part of it—to Jerusalem, Judea, and Samaria and the ends of the earth.

Proclamation is declared by Mark to be the method of mission. The Good News is the message, and the whole world is the scope of the mission.

> He said to them, "Go throughout the whole world and preach the gospel to all mankind. Whoever believes and is baptized will be saved; whoever does not believe will be condemned" (Mark 16:15-16).

Part of the statement reminds one of the blessings and the curses of the ancient suzerainty treaties and elements found in the Old Testament covenant statements.

The commission in Luke conveys this message: preach the death and resurrection of the Messiah in whose name repentance and forgiveness is to be proclaimed to all nations. As in Acts, the disciples are cautioned to wait for the power and are told that their witnessing is to begin in Jerusalem, at home base, and then move out from there.

> Then he opened their minds to understand the Scriptures, and said to them, "This is what is written: the Messiah must suffer and must rise from death three days later, and in his name the message about repentance and the forgiveness of sins must be preached to all nations, beginning in Jerusalem. You are witnesses of these things. And I myself will send upon you what my Father has promised. But you must wait in the city until the power from above comes down upon you" (Luke 24:45-49).

In Luke 1:78-79 is found the Old Testament concept of Israel, personified as a future king, being a light to the Gentiles (Isaiah 9:2-7; 42:5-7; 49:1,5-6).

The mandate to mission in John is different in wording than the other Gospels but contains the commission to go, the empowerment for the mission, and a message of forgiveness of sins. The disciples are sent by Jesus, even as Jesus had been sent by the Father. The empowerment comes through the Holy Spirit breathed on them by Jesus.

> Jesus said to them again, "Peace be with you. As the Father sent me, so I send you." Then he breathed on them and said, "Receive the Holy Spirit. If you forgive people's sins, they are forgiven; if you do not forgive them, they are not forgiven" (John 20:21-23).

Jesus' prayer for his disciples supports the commission to go. He prays for those who will hear and believe and says that their oneness as his followers will, in itself, be a message to the world. The followers' presence in the world is a message, a proclamation that God loves all people. The disciples are sent ". . . in order that the world may know . . ." (John 17:20-23).

Of all the "commissions" described in the Gospels, the one most quoted by members of the church is the one in Matthew known as the Great Commission. It has at least one element different from the others, given in the form of a promise. It states clearly that the commission is in force to the end of the age, the consummation of the age of the new covenant. Jesus undergirded the importance of the Great Commission by emphasizing that all authority in heaven and on earth had been given to him. He is supreme over all of creation, not just the earth.

Jesus' parable of the five, two, one (or five thousand, two thousand, one thousand silver coins) talents in Matthew 25:14-30 teaches about the proper stewardship, or management, of one's resources for producing more, and it also speaks of the report on one's stewardship that must be made at the time of the master's coming. There is a final day at the end of the age when people will report on their stewardship. (Compare this with Luke 20:9-18 and Luke 12:41-48.)

A. R. Fagan has said of the parables of the kingdom:

> In each of them, we see from different perspectives *life being lived in the Kingdom with every relationship and circumstance giving evidence of God's ownership, man's acknowledgement of it, man's acceptance of his accountability, and man's responsible management of God's gifts.* That's biblical stewardship![2]

From the parable of the five, two, and one talents, we should learn that there is no excuse for not producing, even if we have only one talent in hand. Many today are tempted to bury the one talent on the grounds that a talent is such a little thing: "I am only a one-talent person!" However, in those days one talent was worth about $1,000. A day's wage then was about twenty cents. On the basis of a six-day work week, the one talent had the value of almost sixteen years of wages! Regardless of one's income, whether an average wage, Social Security, a pension, or welfare, if there were sixteen years of payments in hand at one time, the amount would be sizeable.

Another parable, Luke 16:1-13, the unrighteous steward (shrewd manager), is not quite so clear about the final day, or the consummation of the age. However, two things Jesus said hint at a final judgment of one's managership, or stewardship: first, he said, "If, then, you have not been faithful in handling worldly wealth, how can you be trusted with true wealth?" and then, "if you have not been faithful to what belongs to someone else, who will give you what belongs to you?" (Luke 16:11-12). Look also at Matthew 13:24-30; Luke 20:9-18; Luke 12:41-48; Matthew 25:1-13; Matthew 13:47-52; Luke 14:15-24.

Parables often have something to say about stewardship. Someone has said that sixteen out of thirty-eight parables are concerned with how to handle money and possessions. In the story of the rich fool (see Luke 12:13-21), one can see that one should make provision for passing on wealth when death occurs, as well as develop a proper attitude toward earthly possessions and the God-human relationship. For, God asked, ". . . then who will get all these things . . . ?''

Some will find in the parable of the good Samaritan (see Luke 10:30-37) the following examples of attitudes concerning resources: (1) What is yours is mine if I can get it (the robbers). (2) What is mine is mine, and I shall keep it that way if I can (the priest and the Levite). (3) What is mine is yours if you need it (the Samaritan). (4) I'll risk something, too, in caring for a seriously wounded person and trust "the Samaritan" to pay me if I spend more than he has given me (the innkeeper).

T. K. Thompson says of the parables:

> The teaching of Jesus concerning the disciples as stewards is set forth in a series of parables in the Synoptic Gospels. The main point of the parables lies in setting the relationship of God and man alongside that of the householder and the servant who was in charge of the estate. God is sovereign; man is responsible to him.[3]

To summarize what the commissions in the Gospels and Acts are saying, the following are noted:

1. Wait for empowerment by the Holy Spirit for the witnessing.

2. Start from where you are (your Jerusalem) and go to the whole world, or to all nations.

3. Recognize Jesus as the focal point of the faith, as the Lord and Sovereign of our lives. The gospel of God—the *kerygma,* the message—is centered in a person, not in an idea, not in an ideal, not in a system of thought (doctrine) or practices, not in a people, not in a place.

> The gospel concerns itself with a Person, the Lord Jesus Christ and man's relationship to Him. . . . This Person is presented to us in the deity-humanity mystery and in the cross-resurrection event. These are four dimensions of the Person apart from which Christ ceases to be the Savior of mankind. This is the objective aspect of the gospel. . . . In order to experience Jesus Christ as Saviour, man must be related to Him in a repentance-faith attitude, and he must appropriate the forgiveness of sins made possible by the sacrificial and substitutionary death and triumphant resurrection of Jesus Christ.[4]

4. Make disciples through witnessing and proclaiming the gospel of

  a) the death and resurrection of the Messiah,

  b) the necessity of repentance for sins, and

c) the fact of forgiveness of sins.

5. Baptize the new disciples, and thereby symbolize the transition from the old life to the new life.

6. Teach the new disciples the way of obedience to the Lord Jesus Christ and his commandments.

Some familiar themes in stewardship are as follows:

1. God is Lord, sovereign. Jesus has all authority.

2. Humans are to live in a responsible relationship to God, which requires caring about other persons.

3. Humans are to practice a stewardship of resources under God the Creator, Lord (Owner), and Redeemer.

4. Resources are to be used in support of the mission of the church.

5. Humans shall give an accounting of their stewardship in this life.

6. There shall be an accounting of stewardship at the final reporting to God.

Questions and Statements for Study and Reflection

1. What is the significance of the resurrection to the mission of the church?

2. How did Jesus see his own mission?
   a) at first
   b) finally

3. Consider the significance of the following two phrases:
   a) ". . . to the ends of the earth" (Acts 1:8)
   b) ". . . to the end of the age" (Matthew 28:20)

4. In what ways do the parables on the kingdom, with their usual reference to the end of time, have an important message in relation to the mission of God's people?

5. In what ways do the parables of Jesus have anything to say about stewardship of resources? (Not every parable has something to say about stewardship.) Study the parables listed below:
   a) The Hidden Treasure, Matthew 13:44
   b) The Pearl of Unusual Quality, Matthew 13:45-46
   c) The Workers in the Vineyard, Matthew 20:1-16

d) The Tenants in the Vineyard, Matthew 21:33-45; Mark 12:1-12; Luke 20:9-18

e) The Ten Girls, Matthew 25:1-13

f) The Rich Man and Lazarus, Luke 16:19-31

g) The Gold Coins, Luke 19:11-27

h) The Steward on Trial, Luke 12:41-48

6. In Jesus' teaching we find the warning against accumulating treasures on earth; for the heart, which is the controlling center of personality, will be where the treasure is. What does such a teaching really mean to us in this modern day? See Matthew 6:19-21; Luke 16:19-31; Luke 16:1-8; Matthew 25:14-30 and Luke 12:16-21. Also, see 1 Timothy 6:17-19 and compare with Luke 16:11-12.

5

CHOSEN TO PROCLAIM
THE WONDERFUL
ACTS OF GOD

Daily Bible Readings

1. Chosen to Proclaim the Wonderful Acts of God
     1 Peter 2:1-10; Acts 10:30-43; Exodus 19:5-6

2. Shine Among Them like Stars
     Philippians 2:12-16; Isaiah 42:6-7; 49:6; Luke 2:32

3. God's Own People in Union with Christ
     Ephesians 1:3-14; 2:11-22

4. All People Are God's Friends Through Jesus Christ
     2 Corinthians 5:14-21; Philippians 2:5-11; Colossians 1:15-23

5. Chosen and Sent to Pass It On
     John 17:18; Acts 13:1-4; 1 Corinthians 11:23-25; 15:1-8

6. Called to Preach the Good News to Everyone
     Acts 16:6-10; Romans 1:1-17; 10:9-17

7. Sharing in the Word of Truth
     Philippians 4:10-18; 3 John, vv. 5-8

CHOSEN TO PROCLAIM THE WONDERFUL ACTS OF GOD
1 Peter 2:9

30 A.D. **Consummation**

Philip: ". . . he told him the Good News about Jesus . . ." (Acts 8:26-39).

Peter: "God has shown me that I must not consider any person ritually unclean or defiled. . . . I now realize that it is true that God treats everyone on the same basis. . . . peace through Jesus Christ, who is Lord of all. . . . the one whom God has appointed judge of the living and the dead . . ." (Acts 10:28-43).

". . . you will serve as holy priests. . . . you are the chosen race, the King's priests, the holy nation, God's own people, chosen to proclaim the wonderful acts of God . . ." (1 Peter 2:5, 9-10; compare with Exodus 19:9-10).

Some of the Wonderful Acts of God:
> Creation and commission to stewardship
> Covenant with Abraham
> Exodus events, from slavery in Egypt to Promised Land
> Return of the Remnant from exile in Babylon
> Jesus—birth, life, death, resurrection
>> (Lord's Supper/Communion/Eucharist)
> Consummation or end of the age, yet to come

Paul: ". . . no such thing as Jew and Greek . . . you are all one person in Christ Jesus . . . 'issue' of Abraham, and so heirs by promise'' (Galatians 3:28-29, NEB).

"Every Sunday each of you must put aside some money, in proportion to what he has earned . . ." (1 Corinthians 16:2).

"They have been severely tested by the troubles they went through; but their joy was so great that they were extremely generous in their giving, even though they are very poor" (2 Corinthians 8:2; read all of chapters 8 and 9).

CHOSEN TO PROCLAIM THE WONDERFUL ACTS OF GOD
1 Peter 2:9

The initial movement of the church in mission was brought about by Saul's persecution of the church in Jerusalem. Being persecuted, scattering to Judea and Samaria, and preaching the message were the Christian experiences of the day.

> And Saul approved of [Stephen's] murder. That very day the church in Jerusalem began to suffer cruel persecution. All the believers, except the apostles, were scattered throughout the provinces of Judea and Samaria. . . . preaching the message (Acts 8:1-4).

The presence of the believers in the provinces brought the Good News to the people who lived there.

One of those scattered believers was Philip. In the principal city of Samaria he preached about the Messiah, Jesus Christ, and the Good News of the kingdom of God. Many believed and were baptized. There was a great joy in that city. Philip's presence on the road from Jerusalem to Gaza brought him into contact with an Ethiopian official who was reading Isaiah 53:7-8 as he rode along in his chariot. The encounter of Philip and the Ethiopian led the Ethiopian to ask about the one of whom the prophet was speaking. Then Philip told him about Jesus of Nazareth. This conversation resulted in the Ethiopian asking to be baptized. After the baptism, the Ethiopian official went on his way rejoicing, and Philip continued preaching the Good News in every city from Ashdod to Caesarea. Philip apparently had had no hesitation about getting into the chariot with an Ethiopian. The official probably was a proselyte to the Jewish faith. He was reading the prophet Isaiah on his way home from Jerusalem when he encountered Philip.

Simon Peter was a disciple who spoke in Caesarea. His statement to the large gathering in the home of Cornelius, a captain in the Roman army regiment called "The Italian Regiment," reveals clearly the normal feeling of the Jewish people toward other races. It also reveals Peter's insight into God's feelings toward non-Jewish people. This is the beginning in the church of a breakthrough for the gospel, a gospel that was intended to be for all nations.

> He said to them, "You yourselves know very well that a Jew is not allowed
> by his religion to visit or associate with Gentiles. . . . I now realize that
> it is true that God treats everyone on the same basis. Whoever fears him
> and does what is right is acceptable to him, no matter what race he belongs
> to" (Acts 10:28-35).

In practice, Peter did not always live up to this revelation and new
insight. We learn of this later in Paul's letter to the Galatians (Galatians
2:11-14) when Paul speaks of having opposed Peter in public for the
way he was acting toward the Gentiles. In this same context Paul speaks
of Peter as apostle to the Jews and himself as apostle to the Gentiles
(Galatians 2:7-10). Apparently Peter had kept his primary ministry
among the Jews.

Some of the scattered believers went as far away as Phoenicia,
Cyprus, and Antioch. Some preached to Jews only. But some believers
from Cyprus and Cyrene also went to Antioch and told the message of
the Good News to the Gentiles (Acts 11:19-20). Barnabas went up to
Antioch from Jerusalem to see what was happening in Antioch where
Jews and Gentiles were together in the church. Following the visit in
Antioch, Barnabas went on to Tarsus to look for Paul. Paul went to
Antioch with Barnabas, and there they taught in the church for a whole
year (Acts 11:22-26). Believers were first called Christians in Antioch.
The Antioch church felt led by the Spirit of God to send Barnabas and
Paul out as missionaries (Acts 13:1-3). The rest of the book of Acts
tells of Paul's missionary journeys—his return to the church in Antioch,
visit in Jerusalem, imprisonment in Caesarea, trip to Rome, and continued imprisonment in Rome.

Soon after his arrival in Rome, Paul called the Jewish leaders together
and explained to them his message about the kingdom of God (Acts
28:23-24). Some of the leaders became believers and some of them did
not. He then declared that they should know that God's message of
salvation had been sent to the Gentiles (Acts 28:28).

Paul was very clear on the point that he was an apostle to the Gentiles
(Galatians 1:15-16a; 3:13-16; and 3:29; Colossians 1:25-29; 1 Timothy
2:3-7; Romans 1:5, 13b, 16-17).

> So there is no difference between Jews and Gentiles, between slaves and
> free men, between men and women; you are all one in union with Christ
> Jesus. If you belong to Christ, then you are descendants of Abraham and
> will receive what God has promised (Galatians 3:28-29).

Here Paul is saying what would have seemed incredible to those who believed that the descent from Abraham was through the Hebrew people. Paul was radically changing values. He was saying that the descent was from Abraham to Jesus Christ to the Gentile world. This change of focus from Israel to the Gentile world is central to God's design for salvation.[1]

This relating of the New Testament events to the Old Testament events, is not, in fact, new to God's design. God has always pointed toward the peoples of the earth as his concern. This concern was first expressed to the world in Genesis 12:1-8. There Abraham was promised that through his descendants a blessing would be provided to all nations. Salvation has always been through faith, and Abraham was a man of faith.

In Galatians 3:29 Paul writes of the promise to Abraham and speaks of the Galatian Gentiles as descendants of Abraham. Paul refers to the Sinai covenant in Galatians 4, speaking of the children of Hagar, a slave woman, and the children of the free woman Sarah. He goes on to relate that the slave woman and her children represent the old covenant made at Mount Sinai and the free woman and her children represent the new covenant. It is almost as if Paul is saying that, as important as the event of Sinai and its covenant are, the really important covenant is the one with Abraham and his descendants by the free woman Sarah. These are the descendants who are to be a blessing to the world. And these descendants include the Gentile people who have faith in God through Jesus Christ (see Romans 4). This same emphasis upon the descendants of Sarah was strongly stressed in Genesis (Genesis 17:15-22). And now Paul is saying that the real descent is by faith, not by natural genealogical descent.

Other references to the Abrahamic covenant in relation to the gospel are made by Peter in his sermon in the temple (Acts 3:11ff.), by Stephen in his speech to the council (Acts 7:1), and by Paul in reference to the sureness of God's promises that Jesus would be a high priest forever (Hebrews 6:13-17) and that salvation would be by faith, just as it was for Abraham (Romans 4–6).

Paul's theology of one people in Christ found expression in a most exciting way when he discussed the offering being taken in the Macedonian churches for the poor church members in Jerusalem. The word Paul used for the contribution was not one primarily used for money.

It was one used to express relationships. The word is transliterated into English from Greek as *koinonia*. Commonality is what this word expresses, the being together in a common experience. The terms *contribution* in 2 Corinthians 9:13 and *contribute* in Romans 15:27 (NEB) are translations of *koinonia*. Paul is saying of Gentile Christians in Greece and of Jewish Christians in Jerusalem, "You are demonstrating your unity, your oneness in the giving and receiving of this offering." Because of this, he exhorts that the *contributions* be generous—positive proof of unity in relationships. J. G. Davies in *Worship and Mission* wrote:

> The collection was a visible demonstration of the truth for which he was struggling. That the Gentile churches should contribute for the poor at Jerusalem was proof positive of the actuality of *koinonia*, that Jew and Gentile were one in Christ. So writing to the Romans, he can say that the Christians of Macedonia and Achaia have made 'a certain *koinonia*, for the poor among the saints that are at Jerusalem' ([Romans] 15:26).[2]

This theological position in relation to the offering puts funding for mission into the spirit of "Partners in Mission," a phrase used by some people when they speak of mission outreach in the twentieth century.

In his letter to the Corinthian church, Paul also spoke of God loving a cheerful giver. When I was a senior in college, three of us visited another church on a Sunday evening and sat in the balcony. Before the offering plate came to us that evening, one of my fellow students said that he had a fifty-cent piece and a five-cent piece. He went on to say that he would give the five-cent piece because God loves a cheerful giver. He couldn't give the fifty-cent piece and be cheerful about it! I have never forgotten that moment. I have never believed that my friend used the biblical text properly but have always believed that God does want us to give cheerfully. How interesting and exciting, as well as instructive, to know that 2 Corinthians 9:7 can be quite properly translated, "God loves a hilarious giver"! Why not? Give with sweet abandon and freedom. Many years later the director of planned giving for a Midwestern church college wrote in the school's alumni paper these words that illustrate giving with joy and freedom:

> I had a very interesting visit with one of our key supporters. His description of the fun of giving . . . "Before we decided to become tithers, we considered each request for support individually. We struggled and agonized over each one and often found decisions hard to make. Once we

decided to tithe, our only consideration was in choosing to whom to give. When it came down to deciding only *where* to give and not *if*, family giving, for us, really became fun!''

Again, when Paul wrote of the offering for the Jerusalem church, he expressed another idea which is sometimes called proportionate giving. Any proportion is a percentage, but there is more to it than a percentage.

Every Sunday each of you must put aside some money, in proportion to what he has earned . . . (1 Corinthians 16:2).

Paul was probably remembering what Moses said on one occasion:

Each man is to bring a gift as he is able, in proportion to the blessings that the LORD your God has given him (Deuteronomy 16:16-17).

(See also 2 Corinthians 8:12; Exodus 35:4-9; Ezra 2:69; Nehemiah 10:37-39; Mark 12:41-44; Acts 11:27-30.)

All giving begins with the tithe. Proportionate giving moves above that as income increases. Perhaps the concept of proportionate spacing on some typewriters will help us to understand. In the case of the typewriter, the amount of space used is based on the size of the letter being typed. A basic space is needed for the lowercase letter *i;* the capital letter *M* needs more space. Every letter uses space but some use more than others. In stewardship, as the income increases, the amount to be given increases. No one is left out. Even the people with small incomes can and need to give. Those with larger incomes can and should give more. To whom much is given, much will be required.

Paul gave instruction to the newly founded churches concerning their support for the founders of the church when he wrote:

Surely you know that the men who work in the Temple get their food from the Temple and that those who offer the sacrifices on the altar get a share of the sacrifices. In the same way the Lord has ordered that those who preach the gospel should get their living from it (1 Corinthians 9:13-14).

Yet, Paul was explicit in saying that he had not asked support for himself from the church at Corinth but had received it from *other* churches while he worked there (2 Corinthians 11:7-9). Paul gave instructions to Titus in Crete regarding support for traveling teachers. They were to be provided everything they needed (Titus 3:13). Through Paul's letter of appreciation written to the church in Philippi we know that they supported him in his missionary travels to preach the Good News (Philippians 4:10-20). He called their gifts a profit to their account. He spoke of their sharing with him in terms of profits and losses, and he described his letter to them as a receipt for everything they had given him.

Paul's call for support of the traveling evangelist, church founder, or missionary is a seldom-used method in twentieth-century mission philosophy. In the twentieth century the missionary is supported by those back home. Some supporting groups insist that the village people must build a house for the teacher to live in if a teacher is to be sent to their village.

The writer of Third John spoke for the support of the traveling missionary when he complimented Gaius for sustaining his fellow Christians and urged that he continue doing so. Such support of the traveling teachers would please God. The call was for Christians to supply this aid because those who traveled "in the service of Christ" would not accept support from unbelievers. Support from believers was considered by the writer as a sharing in ". . . their work for the truth" (3 John, vv. 5-8). In Second John the writer gave a warning not to support a certain false teacher for to do so would be a sharing as "his partner in the evil things he does."

An emphasis in the Bible, in both Old and New Testaments, upon the descendants of Abraham as the people of God is important to remember, for they were to fulfill God's purpose in the world. They were chosen for that task (1 Peter 1:1-2). Later in First Peter there is a more complete formula statement of the purpose of God's people:

> Come as living stones, and let yourselves be used in building the spiritual temple, where you will serve as holy priests to offer spiritual and acceptable sacrifices to God through Jesus Christ.
>
> But you are the chosen race, the King's priests, the holy nation, God's own people, chosen to proclaim the wonderful acts of God, who called you out of darkness into his own marvelous light. At one time you were not God's people, but now you are his people; at one time you did not know God's mercy, but now you have received his mercy (1 Peter 2:5, 9-10).

Compare this with Exodus 19:5-6, and also see 1 Corinthians 15:28; 2 Corinthians 5:17-19; Galatians 6:15-16; and Revelation 1:5b-6. Three of the mighty acts of God often mentioned in the Bible have to do with salvation and freedom: the rescue of the children of Israel from Egypt to residence in the Promised Land (Exodus 13:1-2, 11-16); a new exodus from captivity in Babylon and their return to the Promised Land (Ezra 1:1-4); and the redemptive acts of Jesus in the crucifixion and resurrection with the promise of a more abundant life and ". . . rooms in my Father's house . . . [that] I am going to prepare . . . for you" (John 14:2; see also Romans 1:4). This salvation by Jesus relates to the life that follows this life, as well as to the present life.

The whole biblical story appears to be saying that God's purpose is for all people to be blessed by sharing the Good News about the right relationships with God that are possible, as history moves from the creation of the universe to the consummation of the age. (See Philippians 2 :14-16; Ephesians 1:19*b*-23; 2:10, 14-22; 3:8-11.) The purpose of the church is caught up in God's purpose in history and in powers beyond the earth. History has a goal, and the church has a place in reaching that goal.

The Church as a Sign and First Fruit of the Consummation: Unfinished Creation.[3]

Heaven and earth (this is, all that is) are seen to be a part of the majestic purpose of God which moves in a vast sweep from beginning to end, from Creation to Consummation.[4]

. . . but the purpose of the church is to aid the growth of the cosmos, the development of the universe, to completion and consummation, to the full realization of the kingdom of God. We call this eschatology.[5]

See also 1 Corinthians 1:6-9; 1 Timothy 6:13*b*-16; 1 and 2 Thessalonians; Hebrews 12:22-28 and Matthew 25:31-46.

In the Matthew 25:31-46 selection, the Son of man is said to be coming as king, to be seated on the royal throne, with all the nations gathered before him. Jesus says that this king will say:

"Come, you that are blessed by my Father! Come and possess the kingdom which has been prepared for you ever since the creation of the world" (Matthew 25:34*b*).

The creation, the people of God, the kingdom of God, and the consummation of history are visible in this brief statement of Jesus.

In Hebrews 12:22-28 Jesus is said to have arranged the new covenant, and this new covenant is described as a better covenant (Hebrews 7:22 and 8:6-7). In the closing benediction prayer of the book of Hebrews it is said that the eternal covenant is sealed by Jesus' death (Hebrews 13:20). An Old Testament prophetic theme is that a new covenant will be revealed (Jeremiah 31:31-37). See also Paul's emphasis upon the covenant (2 Corinthians 3:1-8).

Immediately following the Acts 1:8 commission to the disciples to go in mission "to the ends of the earth," Jesus was seen to leave in a cloud with the promise that he would come back "in the same way that you saw him go to heaven" (Acts 1:11b).

The church (God's people) has a mission to go to all nations with the gospel. The Lord of creation and of our faith has with all authority commanded the church to go. Early Christians shared the gospel as they moved about, whether that movement was for change of residence, for business or trade, because of persecution, or for the specific purpose of sharing the faith. Support was sometimes earned by the one going, as Paul did with his tentmaking. In other cases support was given by a newly established church along the route. God's purpose in all of history has been for God's people to share the story of God with other people as history moved from its beginning toward the final days.

A group of twelve men met in a retreat a few years ago for conversation and dialogue with the Dutch theologian Henrik Kraemer. Their question for consideration was "What is the church for?" Their conclusion was very similar to the conclusions reached in the previous paragraph.

> . . . we did agree that the church exists as God's instrument in the world to fulfill God's purposes, which he made known in the Scriptures of both the Old and New Testaments, and the incarnation of Jesus Christ.
>
> It could be said that the story of the Bible, in both Old and New Testaments, testifies to the unchanging purpose of God to give his love to the whole world.[6]

When one thinks about the sweep of history from a biblical perspective and thinks about the general feelings of people in our present world, one can easily come to the conclusion that the greatest danger to effective and joyful stewardship and mission (evangelistic outreach) is the feeling that there is no God or that God is absent from what is going on in the world. Today's question "If there is a God, why . . .?" is not unlike the question of people during the time of Malachi. They asked, "Where is the God who is supposed to be just?" (Malachi 2:17b). God wasn't real and present. In their minds God was so absent from their presence that they thought nothing of bringing blemished animals for the temple offerings and they failed to bring their tithes to the temple. God couldn't see, wouldn't notice, didn't care. But God did care and still does. Our attitude affects our outlook and action.

It is possible for us to look back and then proclaim God's wonderful acts. We can look at the present and the past and be sure that there is a future. God's plan for the ages is to be finished. Let us praise God (see Ephesians 1:3-14).

Let us . . . praise God's glory (Ephesians 1:12).

In all his wisdom and insight God did what he had purposed. . . . *This plan,* which *God will complete* when the time is right, *is to bring all creation together,* everything in heaven and on earth, *with Christ as head* (Ephesians 1:8b-10, emphasis added).

Questions and Statements for Study and Reflection

1. What am I doing to light up the sky through offering the message of life? (presence and proclamation)

2. What is my calling to ministry in God's kingdom?

3. What relationship does the outreach of the church have to the continuing change in the universe? See Morikawa's book *Biblical Dimensions of Church Growth*.

4. List references in the Scripture that state or imply that the believers in Jesus are the new Israel.

5. List elements of the gospel, mission, redemption, and Jesus' glory that you find in these statements in Scripture: Romans 1:1-13,16-17; Romans 10:9; 1 Corinthians 11:23-25;15:3-7; Philippians 2:6-11; Hebrews 1:1-4;1 Peter 3:18-22.

6. Consider the early confession of the church that "Jesus is Lord" (1 Corinthians 12:3).

7. For pleasure, read the Coronation Psalm (Psalm 24) while thinking of Jesus having all authority in heaven and in earth. Read it out loud with considerable feeling.

8. Review your notes on *Daily Bible Readings,* lifting out themes that relate to God's mission for God's people. List these across the top of a sheet or sheets and put under each one a list of the biblical references that refer to the theme. God's mission has to do with both stewardship and outreach.

SELECTED BIBLIOGRAPHY

Anderson, Bernhard W., *The Unfolding Drama of the Bible: Eight Studies Introducing the Bible as a Whole,* 3rd ed. Philadelphia: Fortress Press, 1988.

*Blauw, Johannes, *The Missionary Nature of the Church.* Grand Rapids: Wm. B. Eerdmans Publishing Co., 1974. Paperback.

*Costas, Orlando E., *The Church and Its Mission: A Shattering Critique from the Third World.* Wheaton, Ill.: Tyndale House Publishers, 1975.

*Cunningham, Richard B., *Creative Stewardship.* Nashville: Abingdon Press, 1979.

*Fagan, A. R., *What the Bible Says About Stewardship.* Nashville: Convention Press, 1976.

Goodger, W. Donald, ed., *Spotlighting Stewardship.* Toronto: The United Church of Canada, 1981.

Hall, Douglas John, *The Steward: A Biblical Symbol Come of Age.* New York: Friendship Press for Commission on Stewardship, National Council of the Churches of Christ in the U.S.A., 1982.

Harrison, Everet F., ed., *Baker's Dictionary of Theology.* Grand Rapids: Baker Book House, 1960.

Hillers, Delbert R., *Covenant: The History of a Biblical Idea.* Baltimore: The Johns Hopkins University Press, 1969.

*Keucher, William F., *Main Street and the Mind of God.* Valley Forge: Judson Press, 1974.

*Morikawa, Jitsuo, *Biblical Dimensions of Church Growth.* Valley Forge: Judson Press, 1979.

Neill, Stephen, *The Pelican History of the Church: A History of the Christian Missions,* Vol. 6. New York: Penguin Books, 1987.

*Owens, Owen D., *Stones into Bread?* Valley Forge: Judson Press, 1977.

Pappas, Anthony, *Money, Motivation, and Mission in the Small Church.* Valley Forge: Judson Press, 1989.

Peters, George W., *A Biblical Theology of Missions.* Chicago: Moody Press, 1972.

Rusbuldt, Richard E.; Gladden, Richard K.; and Green, Norman M., Jr., *Local Church Planning Manual.* Valley Forge: Judson Press, 1978.

Sider, Ronald J., ed., *Cry Justice: The Bible Speaks on Hunger and Poverty.* Ramsey, N.J.: Paulist Press, 1980.

_____ , *Rich Christians in an Age of Hunger: A Biblical Study.* Downers Grove, Ill.: Inter-Varsity Press, 1977.

Smith, Louis A., and Barndt, Joseph R., *Beyond Brokenness.* New York: Friendship Press, 1980. (Biblical understanding of mission.)

*Trueblood, Elton, *The Validity of the Christian Mission.* New York: Harper & Row, Publishers, Inc., 1972.

Van Benschoten, A. Q., Jr., *Mission Giving and the Self-Image of Congregations: A Study of American Baptists in Kansas.* Ann Arbor, Mich.: University Microfilms International, 1981. (Order number: 8113588; a D.Min. dissertation/project.)

*Warren, Max, *I Believe in the Great Commission.* Grand Rapids: Wm. B. Eerdmans Publishing Co., 1976.

*Now out of print. May be available in church or public libraries.

NOTES

Introduction

[1] John Bright, *The Kingdom of God, The Biblical Concept and Its Meaning for the Church* (Nashville: Abingdon Press, 1953), p. 10.

[2] Ibid., pp. 232-233.

[3] William J. Keech, *The Life I Owe* (Valley Forge: Judson Press, 1963), p. 20.

[4] National Council of the Churches of Christ in the U.S.A. Commission on Stewardship, March 18, 1964.

[5] Hugh F. Davidson, *Today's Word for Adults, Living the Word* vol. 3, course 3, Session 8, Spring, 1981, part 10 of 16 (American Baptist Churches in the U.S.A., Valley Forge, Pa.), p. 1.

[6] Peter Gordon White, "Christian Stewardship as the Root of Mission," *Journal of Stewardship*, vol. 33 (New York: Commission on Stewardship of the National Council of the Churches of Christ in the U.S.A., 1980), p. 34.

Chapter One

[1] Fred Denbeaux, "Creation," in *A Handbook of Christian Theology*, ed. Marvin Halverson (New York: Meridian Books, Inc., 1958), p. 65.

[2] Tract, "Man! You're In Charge!" Item WSM 718-2-754, © 1971 S&B.

[3] D. J. Hall, "Mission as a Function of Stewardship," in *Spotlighting Stewardship*, ed. W. Donald Goodger (Toronto: The United Church of Canada, 1981), pp. 18-44.

Chapter Two

[1] Delbert R. Hillers, *Covenant: The History of a Biblical Idea* (Baltimore: The John Hopkins University Press, 1969), pp. 29-30.

[2] Stephen Neill, *Christian Missions*, vol. 6 of *The Pelican History of the Church*, ed. Owen Chadwick (New York: Penguin Books, 1964), p. 17.

[3] Hillers, *Covenant*, p. 119.

Chapter Three

[1] Delbert R. Hillers, *Covenant: The History of a Biblical Idea* (Baltimore: The John Hopkins University Press, 1969), pp. 130-131.

[2] Max Warren, *I Believe in the Great Commission* (Grand Rapids: Wm. B. Eerdmans Publishing Co., 1976), pp. 136-137.

[3]Johannes Blauw, *The Missionary Nature of the Church* (Grand Rapids: Wm. B. Eerdmans Publishing Co., 1974. Paperback.), p. 30.

[4]Stephen Neill, *Christian Missions*, vol. 6 of *The Pelican History of the Church*, ed. Owen Chadwick (New York: Penguin Books, 1964), p. 18.

Chapter Four

[1]Johannes Blauw, *The Missionary Nature of the Church* (Grand Rapids: Wm. B. Eerdmans Publishing Co., 1974. Paperback.), pp. 88-89.

[2]A. R. Fagan, *What the Bible Says About Stewardship* (Nashville, Tennessee: Convention Press, 1976), p. 15.

[3]T. K. Thompson, ed., *Stewardship in Contemporary Theology* (Wilton, Conn.: Association Press, 1960), p. 47.

[4]George W. Peters, *A Biblical Theology of Missions* (Chicago: Moody Press, 1972), p. 312.

Chapter Five

[1]Johannes Blauw, *The Missionary Nature of the Church* (Grand Rapids: Wm. B. Eerdmans Publishing Co., 1974. Paperback.), p. 98.

[2]J. G. Davies, *Worship and Missions* (Wilton, Conn.: Association Press, 1967), p. 137.

[3]Jitsuo Morikawa, *Biblical Dimensions of Church Growth* (Valley Forge: Judson Press, 1979), p. 81.

[4]Bernhard W. Anderson, *The Unfolding Drama of the Bible* (Wilton, Conn.: Association Press, 1971), p. 22.

[5]Morikawa, *Biblical Dimensions,* p. 81.

[6]William F. Keucher, *Main Street and the Mind of God* (Valley Forge: Judson Press, 1974), pp. 74, 76.

LEADER'S GUIDE

This Leader's Guide will help a church to grow in its understanding of the biblical basis for stewardship, its planning for programming, and its understanding of mission philosophy in the late twentieth century. The guide is in two segments. Segment one, "Study Guide" for *What the Bible Says About Stewardship,* will assist a leader to plan for a series of lessons based on the textbook. Segment two, "Church Self-Study," will help a church to take a look at itself and plan for future action.

A study for a Doctor of Ministry project and dissertation revealed that in the churches studied there was a need for

1. a greater comprehension of the biblical basis for a theology of mission, a major portion of a Christian's stewardship responsibility;
2. a developed articulateness about the purpose of the church;
3. an enriched understanding of what is happening in the approach to mission in the twentieth century.

When a theology of mission from the whole Bible was discussed, there was considerable surprise about the Old Testament teachings and also a great appreciation for this new awareness. Churches that had written a statement or confession of faith tended to give more for the wider mission. Mission in the late twentieth century has to be conducted differently than in the nineteenth century because the world has changed. Supporters of missions will usually give with greater appreciation when they understand this change.

This textbook and the leader's guide will help a church to understand its broad stewardship responsibility to care for all creation's resources and to share the Good News in mission to all people.

The "Church Self-Study," which follows the "Study Guide," can help a church move toward a better understanding of its self-image and purpose for being. It can be used as a part of the class study mentioned above or used in a full meeting of the church. A more intensive study concerning a church's purpose, objective, and strategies can make use of the *Local Church Planning Manual* by Rusbuldt, Gladden, and Green.

If you wish to study the different approach to missions in this time, secure materials from your own denomination/communion and collect a variety of books on the subject. One of the most interesting books available was written by a person from the Third World: *The Church and Its Mission: A Shattering Critique from the Third World* by Orlando E. Costas. You may be able to obtain a copy from a library and use it for a group study.

STUDY GUIDE
for *What the Bible Says About Stewardship*

The class sessions for this book about the theology of stewardship of resources and mission are arranged into five two-period meetings with a break between the two periods. The guide suggests how the session time may be used. The leader will need to work on an agenda suitable for the group. The agenda may vary from the suggestions provided. If ten one-hour sessions are desired, each of the five outlined sessions may be broken into two sessions. Usually this division will be at the point of the break.

The "Daily Bible Readings" are intended to be read and studied along with the chapter of the text. The themes found in the readings will add information to the material in the chapter.

The "Questions and Statements for Study and Reflection" are sometimes used in suggestions for class work. The leader may wish to use other or additional questions. All together, these resources will help the class members to grow in stewardship understanding.

Session 1

Basis of Session 1: Introduction and Chapter 1

Opening

Worship based on *Stewardship Affirmation 1*

(The affirmations may be found in the "Questions and Statements for Study and Reflection" following the Introduction.)

- Brief comments based on one or more of the listed biblical texts
- An appropriate hymn or gospel song
- Prayer
- Unison reading of the affirmation

Development

1. Make general assignments.

(These two assignments, along with the instructions to read the Introduction and chapter 1, should be duplicated and handed out a week before the first session.)

a) Read the "Daily Bible Readings."

The readings relate to the chapter in the textbook. Sometimes there is an Old Testament and a New Testament selection on the same general idea. Make a record of themes found in the biblical material and watch for repetition of themes. (In a final session of the class, you may provide an opportunity for discussing the themes and how they relate to the stewardship messages of CARE FOR ALL CREATION and MISSION TO ALL PEOPLE.) Following are examples of themes found in the readings for chapter 1, day 2:

Genesis 1:1–2:4a

God created the universe, the heavens, and the earth.

The power of God was manifested in the creating process.

The earth shall be managed by human beings.

God was pleased with the creation.

Revelation 21:1-7

The new creation is in place at the end of time.

The old creation has disappeared.

The Holy City is coming down.

God encompasses all things and makes them new.

Humans have the right to drink the water of life.

The water of life is free.

There is a place of second death.

b) As the text is read, give attention to the "Questions and Statements for Study and Reflection."

Some of these may be used for special assignments and reports.

2. Make special assignments.

   a) Enlist one or two people to prepare an "Affirmation of Mission" and develop a worship service for Session 5. The four stewardship affirmations are a model for the "Affirmation of Mission."

   b) Enlist a class member to prepare a report on the meaning of "covenant" to present at Session 2.

   c) Have someone prepare a report on the tithe for Session 2, especially as its meaning relates to Abraham and Jacob. Hold for Session 3 the tithe material from other Old Testament references (including Malachi), what Jesus had to say about tithing, and what Paul had to say about proportionate giving.

   d) Assign two or three persons to prepare to discuss in front of the class in Session 2 the meaning of being a priest.

   e) Consider the theology of the treatment of the poor as found in the Bible and have members report it in Session 2. Among other sources, see *Cry Justice: The Bible Speaks on Hunger and Poverty,* by Ronald J. Sider, and *Stones into Bread? What Does the Bible Say About Feeding the Hungry Today?* by Owen D. Owens.

   f) Have two or three members prepare to discuss in front of the class in Session 2 the meaning of the Exodus event—to the Hebrews and to the Christians.

3. Review the Introduction and chapter 1.

4. Do numbers 1 and 2 of the "Questions and Statements for Study and Reflection" for the Introduction. Share responses with one another. Plan to do this again in Session 5 and compare the two sets of responses.

(Break)

5. Discuss the meaning of being put in charge of the whole creation and relate this to the phrase "having dominion" found in the King James Version of the Bible.

6. Note similarities and differences of being put in charge (Genesis 1) and taking care of the Garden of Eden (Genesis 2).

7. Write on newsprint the response to number 2 of chapter 1, "Questions and Statements for Study and Reflection." The attitudes and continuing response to this area of interest may be the most important late-twentieth-century stewardship emphasis.

8. As a group, discuss numbers 3 through 5 of the "Questions and Statements" at the end of chapter 1.

Concluding Moments

Discuss the stewardship implications of the editorial "The Way of the Tree" found at the end of chapter 1.

Session 2

Basis of Session 2: Chapter 2
Opening
Worship based on *Stewardship Affirmation 2*

Use an order of worship similar to that used in Session 1. The leader may do it or may enlist members to lead the worship.

Development

1. Leader reviews chapter 2.
2. Report on the meaning of "covenant" and follow that with a class discussion.
3. Report on the tithe as assigned.
4. Report on the Exodus event and follow with class discussion.

(*Break*)

5. Assigned persons discuss in front of the class the meaning of being a priest. Then the class members discuss the concepts, especially as they relate to evangelism/mission today.
6. Consider the theology of the treatment of the poor.

Concluding Moments

Identify one way the church can be in ministry to the poor in addition to what it is already doing. Make plans to do that ministry.

Session 3

Basis of Session 3: Chapter 3
Opening
Worship based on *Stewardship Affirmation 3*

Use an order of worship similar to that used in previous worship periods. The leader may enlist members to lead the worship.

Development

1. Make assignment for Session 4.
   Study the parables as indicated in "Questions and Statements" at the end of chapter 4. Be prepared to discuss teachings on stewardship found in the listed parables.
2. Share insights on stewardship of resources and mission found in the thinking of the prophets (see chapter 3).

3. Dialog on the prophets' messages regarding stewardship of resources and mission.
4. List any words from the prophets that give special significance to Abraham and God's covenant with him.

(Break)

5. Finish the report on tithing in the Old Testament including the information found in Malachi, what Jesus said about tithing, and what Paul said on proportionate giving.
6. In what ways does social concern relate to salvation? Look carefully at the latter part of the Book of Isaiah.

Concluding Moments

Do any activities planned for the first two sessions which you did not have time to do. List on newsprint any stewardship subject about which the members have a special concern. Indicate which ones are not already in your plans for coming sessions. Discuss these together and, if necessary, ask persons to come prepared to discuss them further in Session 4. Insofar as possible all the interests of class members should be covered in the five sessions.

Session 4

Basis of Session 4: Chapter 4

Opening

Worship based on *Stewardship Affirmation 4*

Use an order of worship similar to that used in previous sessions.

Development

1. Assign 2 Corinthians 8–9 to be studied for insights on stewardship. These insights will be reported and discussed at Session 5.
2. Review chapter 4.
3. Hold a discussion on stewardship findings found in the parables. Be sure to include any teachings on mission outreach or evangelism. Write the findings on newsprint where they can be seen by the class.
4. Discuss the significance of the resurrection in relation to the mission of the church.

(Break)

5. Look at item 6 in "Questions and Statements" following chapter 3 and discuss it.

Concluding Moments

Using a felt-tip pen, write the following words and phrases on 3″ x

5″ cards, one word or phrase on each card:

water	birds
tame animals	minerals
heavens	celestial bodies
environment	fish
wild animals	dirt
earth	space
seas	rivers
percentage giving	nuclear wastes
proportionate giving	body organs (heart, kidney, etc.)
chemical waste	chemical waste dumps
mercy	medicine
money	mission
compassion	love mercy
oceans	least of these my brothers
offering	tithe
poor	food
altar	hospitals
commitment	do justice
pledges	faithful
war	walk humbly with God
witness	

Have a pen and extra 3″ x 5″ cards available so that additional words or phrases can be added by the class members. Arrange the cards under two general stewardship categories—CARE FOR ALL CREATION and MISSION TO ALL PEOPLE. If any cards do not seem to fit these categories, lay them aside. Now, arrange the cards from top to bottom on the basis of the priority in which the items need attention. If cards seem to be equal in priority, place them side by side. Finally, select the top three cards in each category and make plans for action on these subjects, both at a personal level and at a church level.

Session 5

Basis of Session Five: Chapter 5
Opening
Worship based on the new "Affirmation of Mission" prepared by members of the class.

Development
1. Review chapter 5.
2. Repeat items 1 and 2 of the "Questions and Statements" following chapter 1 and compare the responses with what was written and discussed previously. Note any growth in understanding.
3. Share the findings in 2 Corinthians 8–9. Write the insights on newsprint so that it is visible to the whole group.
4. Discuss the repeated themes discovered in "Daily Bible Readings" and the significance of these.

(Break)

Concluding Moments
1. If desired, conduct a "Church Self-Study." The necessary materials follow this study guide and provide instructions, including a form to reproduce.
2. If you choose not to use the "Church Self-Study," itemize on newsprint the stewardship insights learned during the sessions that seem especially important to the class. List items still needing attention. Consider possible stewardship programming that the church needs to do.

CHURCH SELF-STUDY

The congregation may use this self-study process in a planned general session of the church for the purpose of securing a wide participation of the church members. It also may be used by a smaller study group. The first procedure will assure the church of a widely experienced consciousness raising about its own self-image and will facilitate input from the members for changing its mission self-image.

To begin the self-study process, divide the congregation into small groups of eight to ten people. Circulate forms to be filled out. A leader will need to provide the following information: congregation attendance figures for Section A, statistical data for Section D, and denominational places of mission for Section H. (For Section H, list the places as noted and include two or three places *not* served.) In the small groups each individual will fill out his/her own form but with the freedom to talk to others in the group. The dialogue will be beneficial to group understanding. A plenary session should follow in order to share some of the findings and thinking of the small groups. Record the sharing on news-print.

Following the plenary session a small committee of three or four persons can tabulate the forms filled out by the members. This tabulation and the sharing in the plenary session will be the basis for a report to the church as to how the church sees itself as a mission-minded church. The committee will also offer suggestions for church decisions and educational experience that will help move the church from where it is to where it wishes to be.

Following this document as a guide, develop a church self-study instrument suitable for use in your local congregation/church in its denominational/communion structure.

Guide for Church Self-Study on Its Mission Self-Image

A. Name of the Church_____

Address_____

City_____State_____Zip_____

Pastor_____

Associate Pastor_____

Total Membership_____

Resident Membership_____

Average Attendance in Church School_____

Average Attendance in Morning Worship_____

Average Attendance in Evening·Worship_____

Average Attendance in Midweek Service_____

B. Our Budget Style
(Check the appropriate statements.)

( ) The church's wider mission giving is the total of giving by the individual members for mission beyond the local community.

( ) We ask for separate pledges for the local mission (maintenance and ministry of the church in the local community) and for the wider mission.

( ) The church budgets a dollar amount for missions, one-twelfth of which is sent each month to the denomination.

( ) Members make one annual pledge to the church, and the church budget specifies the amount for the local mission and for the wider mission.

( ) An established percentage of undesignated church receipts is sent each month for the wider mission.

( ) In addition, this percentage will increase by one percent of the total receipts each year until a predetermined percentage goal is reached.

C. Missions We Support
(Check the appropriate items.)

( ) Local community missions in addition to support for the church itself

( ) (the name of your own area, state, or region)

( ) (the name of your denomination) mission budget

( ) Other, nondenominational mission budgets

D. Wider Mission Giving Record of the Church
Fill in the dollar figures on the following chart (from your church records) and figure the percentages of increase or decrease.

Fill in the available consumer price indexes and figure the percentage of change. The consumer price indexes are available in the *Monthly Labor Review* and in *U.S. News and World Report.*

Years	1967	1972	1977	1978	1979	1980	1981	1982	1983
Dollars									
% of Gain									
Consumer Price Index	100	125.3	181.5	195.4	219.4	246.8	272.4		
% of Gain		+25.3	+44.9	+7.7	+11.2	+13.5	+8.9		

How do you interpret the performance of your church in relation to the economic trend—falling behind, forging ahead, or keeping even?

Make your observations here:

E. Our Structures for Promotion of Mission(s)
Yes   No (Check the appropriate column.)

( ) ( ) We have a board of missions.

( ) ( ) We have a committee to promote annual mission offerings.

( ) ( ) We have a committee on education for missions.

( ) ( ) Women emphasize missions.

( ) ( ) Men emphasize missions.

( ) ( ) There is a stewardship or finance committee for budgeting and securing funding by an every-member canvass.

F. Ways We Promote Missions
Yes   No (Check the appropriate column.)

( ) ( ) We use the materials provided and promote the (name of denomination/communion) mission budget.

( ) ( ) We have a planned, year-round stewardship and missions program.

( ) ( ) The pastor preaches missionary sermons.

( ) ( ) The pastor uses mission illustrations in his or her sermons.

( ) ( ) We encourage members to make contacts and develop relationships with missionaries.

( ) ( ) We encourage members to consider full-time service as vocational church workers.

( ) ( ) We have adopted a policy on the mission of our church.

( ) ( ) We keep this policy on the mission of our church before the membership regularly.

( ) ( ) We do not have such a mission policy. We should develop one.

( ) ( ) We pray regularly for missionaries by name.

( ) ( ) We have artifacts around the church as a reminder of our worldwide mission involvement.

( ) ( ) We have a church library or some other method of keeping mission reading material before the congregation.

G. Observations About Our Theology of Mission

Yes   No (Check the appropriate column.)

( ) ( ) We have recently studied the biblical text to clarify our understanding of the mission of the church.

( ) ( ) We have not made such a study of the biblical text but will plan to do so during the next twelve months.

( ) ( ) We have studied some books and other material on the current situation of missions in our time.

( ) ( ) We have not made such a study of the current situation but will plan to do so soon.

( ) ( ) We understand the meaning of the term "internationalization of missions" and the similar term "partners in mission."

Note: Two possible books that can be used in a study of the biblical nature of missions and missions in our time are *The Missionary Nature of the Church* by Johannes Blauw and *The Church and Its Mission: A Shattering Critique from the Third World* by Orlando E. Costas (check local libraries).

H. Recognition Exercise

In which places does (your denomination/communion name) support mission work where missionaries are present or contribute funds to the national church where no missionaries are present? You may check your answers with one another and in (your denomination/communion book), which lists places of mission.

( )	( )	( )
( )	( )	( )
( )	( )	( )
( )	( )	( )
( )	( )	( )
( )	( )	( )

I. Some Marks of a Mission-minded Church Observable in Our Church

Yes   No (Check the appropriate column.)

(   ) (   ) Has interest in wider mission beyond the need of self-preservation

(   ) (   ) Gives between 20 and 25 percent of total undesignated receipts for the wider mission

(   ) (   ) Gives increasing percentage of receipts to the wider mission

(   ) (   ) Gives consistently high percentage of receipts to the wider mission

(   ) (   ) Gives a high per capita dollar figure to the wider mission, thirty dollars and up

(   ) (   ) Has a strong emphasis upon the biblical mandate for mission

(   ) (   ) Talks about and prays for missionaries by name

(   ) (   ) Has had young people enlist for vocational ministry during the last five years

(   ) (   ) Has provision in the constitution for giving direction to mission education and promotion in the church

J. Describing Our Mission Self-Image

On the basis of answers to the above material, describe the image of your church as to its commitment to mission and the image you would like the church to have eighteen months from now.

(1) The church's commitment to mission now:

(2) The desired image eighteen months from now:

K. Designing a Program to Reach the Desired New Image

Outline things you would like to see done by the congregation during the next two years that would help the church's understanding of its mission, deepen its commitment to mission, affect its perception of itself as a mission-minded body, and increase its giving to the wider mission. Try to project a time schedule for implementing your ideas and strategies.